REACHING TO GOD

REACHING TO GOD

THE CHRISTMAS EDITION

R. A. MATHEWS

The author obtained permission for the use of names and events in this book. Otherwise, all the characters, dialogue, and events herein are completely fictional, and any resemblance to actual persons, living or dead, or to actual dialogue or events is entirely coincidental and unintended. Fictional characters, dialogue, and events have been introduced in the spirit of Jesus's parables and should not be construed as real unless otherwise stated.

Copyright © 2024, 2025 by R.A. Mathews

Book Cover Copyright © 2024 by R.A. Mathews

First Edition 12222025fxd

Paperback ISBN: 978-1-936851-19-5

Hardback ISBN: 978-1-936851-18-8

All rights reserved.

No part of this book or cover may be reproduced in any form or by any electronic or mechanical means, including information storage and retrieval systems, without written permission from the author, except for the use of brief quotations in a book review.

Scripture quotations marked (NASB) are taken from the New American Standard Bible (NASB).

Copyright © 1960, 1962, 1963, 1968, 1971, 1972, 1973, 1975, 1977, 1995 by the Lockman Foundation. Used by permission. **www.Lockman.org**

Scripture quotations marked (NIV) are taken from the Holy Bible, New International Version ® NIV ®. Copyright © 1973, 1978, 1984, 2011 by Biblica, Inc. TM

Used by permission of Zondervan. All rights reserved worldwide. **www.zondervan.com**

The "NIV" and "New International Version" are trademarks registered in the United States Patent and Trademark Office by Biblica, Inc. TM.

Scripture quotations marked (ESV) are from the ESV® Bible (The Holy Bible, English Standard Version®), copyright © 2001 by Crossway, a publishing ministry of Good News Publishers. Used by permission. All rights reserved. May not copy or download more than 500 consecutive verses of the ESV Bible or more than one half of any book of the ESV Bible.

Scripture quotations marked (NLT) are taken from the Holy Bible, New Living Translation, copyright ©1996, 2004, 2007, 2013, 2015 by Tyndale House Foundation. Used by permission of Tyndale House Publishers, Inc., Carol Stream, Illinois 60188. All rights reserved.

To
My Mom and Dad
Who Gave Me Everything

To
My Brother
David Anderson Mathews, III
The Finest Christian I Will Ever Know

ABOUT THE AUTHOR

The Rev. R.A. Mathews is an acclaimed theologian and the author of the *Reaching to God* series, which contains both inspiring stories from the Bible and little-known Scripture. Each text contains footnotes leading the reader to supporting verses in the Bible.

Rev. Mathews graduated from the highest-ranked Baptist seminary in the nation with a Master of Divinity degree and four years of graduate study. Thereafter, she completed extensive, independent Bible research from 2015 to 2024.

Mathews is an award-winning writer, and her weekly articles about the Lord have been published nearly 7,000 times in newspapers across the U.S.

Mathews completed her university education at the age of 21 and started seminary that same year. She then sought ordination and was examined and approved by a panel of pastors and the Association of American Baptist Churches to which her church belongs. She is perhaps the first Baptist woman to receive such an ordination in the South.

The Rev. Mathews subsequently worked in Christian broadcasting and in local churches, preaching and working with children and youth.

Like the Apostle Paul, she is bi-vocational, having graduated from a top-ten-ranked law school with an American Jurisprudence Award in mediation. She mediates disputes and represents children and the mentally challenged.

Mathews also writes fiction under her pen names, Red Mathews and I.C. Ford. She says, "Those who disdain fiction forget that Jesus loved the power of a story. Think of all His parables—The Sower and the Seed, The Prodigal Son, The Good Samaritan, and many more. That's because Jesus knew a story could change a heart."

Mathews is the granddaughter of the Rev. Cora Hughes, a holy woman and ordained Nazarene minister.

"I was reared in a family that dearly loved the Lord," she says, "and I gained a deep understanding of Him early on. I definitely had a head start on my spiritual path.

"The Lord is my all, as you will see. I hope these teachings about Him comfort and strengthen your soul as they have mine."

CONTENTS

Directory of Christmas Events	xv
Come Close to God	1
Love, Joy, Peace, Patience . . .	5

LOVE

The Love of God   9
Endures Forever

1. A FAVORITE CHRISTMAS   11
Two Young Mechanics

2. THE CHRISTMAS EVENTS   19
At-A-Glance

3. THE GREATEST GIFT   35
The Gift You Must Have This Christmas

4. WHEREVER YOU GO   43
He Lived A Life of Adventure

JOY

Joy to the World   53
The Lord Has Come

5. MARY AND ELIZABETH   55
Two Women Who Celebrate Before Christmas

6. CAESAR AUGUSTUS   67
God Goes BIG for His Son's Birthday

7. JOSEPHUS   81
A Thumb on the Scale

8. MICAH'S PROPHECY   87
Oh Little Town of Bethlehem

9. THE SHEPHERDS   93
The World's Greatest Treasure Hunt

10. THE SWADDLING CLOTHS   101
A Coincidence or the Hand of God?

11. THE OLD MAN OF CHRISTMAS   109
The Naughty or Nice List

12. ANNA   117
Like Father, Like Daughter

13. THE MAGI   125
A Star, a Manger, and Gifts

PEACE

The Peace of Jesus   139
Born To a War-Torn Judea

14. THE WARS   141
A City in Distress

15. JOSEPH   151
Ready for God to Show You the Future?

PATIENCE

For a Bajillion Years   161
God Waited Patiently to Bring Us His Son

16. MIND NUMBING OR AWE INSPIRING?   163
Jesus's Family Photograph.

17. BOAZ & RUTH   173
He Just Wanted To Help Her

18. AGE OLD GIFTS   181
The Prophecies of Christmas

LOOKING DEEPER

19. THE EDOMITES   193
Taking a Step Back

20. THEOPHILUS   203
Why Does Luke Omit the Magi?

21. THE PROPHETESS 215
Was It a Tribute?

22. EGYPT 225
The Sojourn in Egypt

SIX GIFTS

What Was Given To Me, I Give To You 233

1. AN UNEXPECTED GIFT 235
Which Would You Choose?

2. THE GIFT OF HEALING 243
This Is Not About Spaghetti

3. THE GIFT OF MAGIC 249
Gomer Pyle God Blessings

4. THE GIFT OF HOPE 257
Miracles Must Be Remembered

5. THE GIFT OF SONG 267
My Mom's Magic

6. THE GIFT OF JOY 275
You Will Find Joy

THE LIGHT

REJECTED GIFTS 285
Mud Pies & Squashed Sandwiches

THE CHRISTMAS QUIZ ANSWERS

Revisiting the Two Young Mechanics 295

Also by R.A. Mathews 305
Acknowledgments 308

CHRISTMAS SCRIPTURE

Matthew's Gospel 311
Matthew Chapters 1 - 2, NASB
Luke's Gospel 317
Luke 1:1 - 2:40, NASB

DIRECTORY OF CHRISTMAS EVENTS

1. The Genealogy of Jesus - Matthew 1:1-17
See Chapter 16

2. A Greeting to Theophilus - Luke 1:1-4
See Chapter 20

3. Gabriel Announces the Birth of John the Baptist - Luke 1:5-25
See Chapter 5

4. Gabriel Visits Mary - Luke 1:26-38
See Chapter 5

5. Mary Lives with Her Relatives for Three Months - Luke 1:39-56
See Chapter 5

6. Zechariah Prophesies After the Birth of John - Luke 1:57-80
See Chapter 18

7. Joseph Learns Mary is with Child - Matthew 1:18-25
See Chapter 4

8. Caesar Augustus Orders a Roman Census - Luke 2:1-3
See Chapter 6

9. Jesus is Born in Bethlehem - Luke 2:4-20
See Chapters 8, 9, 10

10. Jesus is Circumcised and Presented at the Temple - Luke 2:21-40
See Chapters 11, 12

11. The Magi Arrive and the Flight to Egypt - Matthew 2:1-18
See Chapters 13, 14, 15, 20

12. The Death of Herod and Return to Nazareth - Matthew 2:19-23
See Chapters 4, 22

COME CLOSE TO GOD

Is this Book for You?

If you're looking for a Christmas book to learn general facts about the birth of Jesus, perhaps to strengthen your trivia game (no shame there) or for a 50-minute lesson to share with your Sunday school class during the holidays, this book is not your best bet.

You can find a much shorter text that will cover the basics faster.

This is an in-depth study. It's also a book about faith.

Nothing Is Impossible for God

Those who have read my other works know that I focus on every word of Scripture. But my hope is always to offer you more.

The Christmas story is filled with messages of comfort and hope. The birth of Jesus brims with this great truth:

"Nothing is impossible for God."

People in the Christmas story, faced with massive challenges, will show you their walk with the Lord, inspiring you to trust Him and keep moving forward.

We all face adversity—times filled with hardship and fear. Where you turn makes all the difference.

Like the Apostle Paul, a tentmaker and missionary, I am also bi-vocational: lawyer and theologian.

Believe me, they go hand in hand. Yesterday, I had a hearing with a man who had drunk a pint of antifreeze. I was there to protect his rights, but I offered him more.

We sat and I told him what God could do for him, that the Lord is real, that if he would lift his head to God and pray and believe, the Lord would guide his life.

"Draw near to God and He will draw near to you."[1]

The chapters in this book are meant to do just that—bring you closer to God. Key Bible passages repeat again and again in this Christmas book, like Micah's prophecy concerning Bethlehem or the arrival of the Magi in Jerusalem.

These events are important to more than one message. In fact, by the time you finish this book, I doubt you'll ever forget the prophet Micah or Luke's tribute to Anna.

Prophecy and Historical Events

There is often prophecy or historical moments behind Biblical events, and that is surely true when the Lord was born. This text examines those little-known details.

For example, Herod the Great was once aligned with Marc Antony and Cleopatra. Yet Herod survived that disastrous alliance, going on to be titled "King of the Jews" by Rome.

That title, Herod's background, and Herod's relationship with Rome greatly shape the Christmas story.

A Deeper Study

---

1. James 4:8, ESV

For those who want to examine the intricacies of the Bible, there's a look at the Edomites and how they impact the Christmas story.

There's a long chapter on why Luke excludes the Magi. It also examines why Luke, the historian, doesn't mention the "Slaughter of the Innocents," what the murders of the children in and around Bethlehem came to be called.

There's also a discussion on why Luke chose to close his Christmas passage with the prophetess Anna. She's an obscure woman few Christians remember, and yet she's likely a more important figure than we realize, who had a tragic death.

Six Gifts

Since it's Christmas, you will find six gifts God has given to me.

They are not about the Christmas story, and you can see a few of them in previous *Reaching to God* volumes.

Nevertheless, I wanted you to have all of them now because each one changed my life. As I said, they are gifts from God!

I now give them to you.

The Christmas Quiz

At the outset, Chapter 1 contains a Christmas quiz so you can ponder what you recall about the Christmas story. The answers are near the end of this book, if you want to jump ahead.

At-A-Glance Events

Many don't realize that the Christmas story is only in the Gospels of Matthew and Luke. Mark and John don't tell us anything at all about Jesus's birth.

Chapter 2 has an At-A-Glance Chart of events in Matthew's Gospel and in Luke's Gospel, which gives you a quick summary of what each Gospel writer told us.

But their accounts of the birth of Jesus are different, so I added a combined listing of events to show you a way to piece those Gospel stories together. There's a brief one and a detailed one with verses.

Reflection Pages

At the end of most chapters, you will find a place to write notes, revelations, and prayers. I encourage you to date them.

Many will return to this Christmas book year after year and see different things at different times. There's a lot here!

Each year, you may see parts of the story you missed before. You may also see how you've grown in your walk with the Lord over time.

It can be really inspiring.

Scripture

At the end of this book, you'll find the Christmas story as it appears in Matthew and Luke's Gospels. While you read the book, you'll always be able to turn to those Scripture pages and look at Christmas as God wrote it.

I'm not perfect. This book is filled with hundreds of footnotes. Read the Scripture. If you think I'm mistaken, challenge me at RAMathews.com.

I welcome your thoughts.

The Lord is my joy and my peace.
I hope the same for you.
We take this voyage together.

R.A. Mathews
Christmas, 2024

LOVE, JOY, PEACE, PATIENCE . . .

LOVE

Psalm 136

"Give thanks to the Lord, for He is good . . .
It is He who remembered us in our low estate . . .
Give thanks to the God of heaven,
for His steadfast love endures forever."[1]

Jesus said:
". . . abide in my love."[2]

---

1. Psalm 136, ESV
2. **John 15:9**

THE LOVE OF GOD
ENDURES FOREVER

1. A FAVORITE CHRISTMAS

TWO YOUNG MECHANICS

"And the angel said to them, 'Do not be afraid; for behold, I bring you good news of great joy.'"

Luke 2:10[1]

---

1. NASB

TWO YOUNG MECHANICS

It was a chilly December day, but the gas station waiting area was heated—a space not much bigger than a tiny bedroom.

Against a big glass window, facing out over the gas pumps, stood a desk with a cash register. A huge television mounted overhead broadcast a sports event.

Against the opposite wall stood a long couch.

That was the entirety of the room.

I sat there waiting for my car to be repaired.

This station is always busy and has a group of mechanics. Two sat beside me—young guys in their twenties, both taking a break from the cold garage.

It was Christmas week, 2016.

Scripture devotes just three and a half chapters of the Bible to the events surrounding the birth of Jesus. As I said earlier, Mark and John don't discuss the Christmas story at all. Only the historian Luke and Jesus's disciple Matthew tell us about the birth of our Lord.

Those few chapters cover two or three years, from fifteen months before the birth of Christ until perhaps six months or a year after.

But this is debated.

The two young mechanics looked as you would expect—soiled

uniforms, heavy boots, grease under their nails. Remember, there was a large screen TV in that little room, turned to a sports event. It was there for customers and to entertain the mechanics on breaks.

Yet their interest was fixed on the town's newspaper. They held it open between them, both leaning over it, reading together.

But mostly they were thinking and talking, trying to decide the answers to Christmas questions there.

My questions.

At the time, I had been writing weekly articles on Scripture for the newspaper for about a year and a half. And I had an idea for Christmas.

A pop quiz.

I wanted to see if readers would like to answer questions about the Christmas story, enjoying seeing how much they knew.

It worked!

The two saw me, but neither asked me anything, returning their attention to the questions in the newspaper. They talked freely with one another, sharing what they knew about those three and a half chapters of Scripture, quickly eliminating answers that were clearly wrong.

And they took their time.

The two slowly worked through the more difficult possible answers for each question, carefully finding Biblical reasons to eliminate the wrong ones.

I watched them closely. I'll explain why at the end of this book.

Here are some of the questions I asked in 2016, and I added a few more. In that newspaper article, I gave the answers immediately after each question. In this book, the answers are near the end of the text in a chapter called "The Christmas Quiz Answers."

You may find that it's a lot more fun to read all the chapters and then take the quiz again and see if you can narrow the choices to the right answer on your own.

Whatever you decide, **circle your answers in pencil**.

Next year, and for years to come, you may want to take the quiz again. You'll be glad you can start fresh without the answers having been permanently marked.

LOVE

Question 1

What happened 15 months before the birth of Jesus that kicks off the Christmas story?
1. The angel Gabriel speaks to Mary.
2. The angel Gabriel speaks to a priest.
3. An angel appears in a dream to Joseph.
4. All of the above

Consider your answers carefully and make your choice in pencil.

Question 2

When the angel Gabriel spoke to Mary, telling her she would give birth, what else did Gabriel say to her?
1. To name her son Jesus
2. That the baby would be the Son of God
3. That the Holy Spirit would come upon her
4. All of the above

Consider your answers carefully and make your choice in pencil.

Question 3

According to Scripture, after Gabriel appeared to Mary, how did she feel and what did she decide to do first?
1. She was afraid and only told Joseph.
2. She was confused and spent time alone in prayer.
3. She hurried south and spent three joyous months with relatives.
4. None of the above

Consider your answers carefully and make your choice in pencil.

Question 4

Why did Mary and Joseph suddenly travel to Bethlehem when Mary was nine months pregnant?
1. Herod had ordered them to move.

2. Caesar Augustus had ordered a count of his kingdom.
3. Julius Caesar wanted to tax all the inhabitants of Rome.
4. The angel Gabriel told them to go.
5. None of the above

Consider your answers carefully and make your choice in pencil.

Question 5

When Magi came from the East to see Jesus, they stopped first in Jerusalem and asked where they could find the newborn King of the Jews. What happened in the city?
1. Everyone rejoiced and awaited their return.
2. Everyone was troubled.
3. Everyone followed the Magi to Bethlehem.
4. None of the above

Consider your answers carefully and make your choice in pencil.

Question 6

Following the Law of Moses, Jesus was presented at the temple forty days after His birth, and a sacrifice was offered. Who did Mary and Joseph meet when they were at the temple?
1. Herod the Great and his soldiers
2. Simeon, a righteous man, and Anna, the prophetess
3. The Apostle Paul
4. John the Baptist

Consider your answers carefully and make your choice in pencil.

Question 7

Herod the Great killed all the male infants in and around Bethlehem. He lived during the Civil War in Rome. Did he side with:
1. Octavian, who became Caesar Augustus, and Marc Antony
2. Cleopatra and Pharaoh
3. Julius Caesar

LOVE

4. Pontius Pilate
5. None of the above

Consider your answers carefully and make your choice in pencil.

Question 8

Luke does not include the Magi in his Gospel, but he does tell us a huge clue as to when the Magi arrived. What is that little detail, nearly hidden in the Christmas story?

1. Jesus wore a gold ring when He was presented at the temple.
2. Mary and Joseph told Simeon about the Magi.
3. Simeon said he had seen the Magi.
4. Mary and Joseph offered turtledoves or young doves when Jesus was presented at the temple.

Consider your choices and select your answer in pencil.

Question 9

According to Scripture, how many Magi came from the East to see Jesus?

1. One
2. Three
3. One hundred
4. None of the above

Consider your choices and lock in your answer in pencil.

As I said, the answers to these questions are near the end of the book in a section called "The Christmas Quiz Answers."

The next chapter lists the Christmas events in an "At-A-Glance" chart, and that will jog your memory quite a bit.

2. THE CHRISTMAS EVENTS

AT-A-GLANCE

"Therefore the Lord Himself will give you a sign: Behold, the virgin will conceive and give birth to a son, and she will name Him Immanuel."

Isaiah 7:14[1]

---

1. NASB

AT-A-GLANCE
CHRISTMAS EVENTS

FOUR TIMELINES

No one knows exactly how the Gospel Christmas stories fit together, but I have given you my best guess. This chapter contains:

1. "At-A-Glance Events" for Matthew's Gospel.
2. "At-A-Glance Events" for Luke's Gospel.
3. "A Brief Combined Timeline."
4. "A Combined Timeline with Verses."

Matthew's* Events At-A-Glance

1. The genealogy of Jesus. 1:1-17 (* NASB version)

2. The Virgin Mary, betrothed to Joseph, is found to be pregnant by the Holy Spirit. 1:18

3. Joseph plans to send Mary away secretly so she won't be disgraced. 1:19

4. In a dream, an angel of the Lord tells Joseph that the Child was conceived by the Holy Spirit. 1:20

5. Joseph is told to name him Jesus for He will save His people from their sins. 1:21

6. Joseph awakes and does as the angel of the Lord commanded and takes Mary as his wife. 1:24

7. Jesus is born in Bethlehem of Judea in the days of Herod the King. 1:25-2;1

8. Magi arrive from the East, asking where the King of Jews was born, that they saw His star in the East, and have come to worship Him. 2:1-2

9. Herod is troubled, and all of Jerusalem is troubled. 2:3

10. Herod gathers the chief priests and scribes to learn where the Messiah was to be born, and they say Bethlehem. 2:4-6

11. Herod secretly meets with the Magi to determine the exact time the star appeared. 2:7

12. Herod sends the Magi to Bethlehem, telling them to report after they find Him. 2:8

13. The magi leave Jerusalem, the star goes ahead of them, and it stops where the Child is. 2:9

14. The Magi are warned in a dream not to return to Herod and leave for their country a different way. 2:12

15. After the Magi are gone, an angel of the Lord appears to Joseph in a dream and says to get up and flee to Egypt and stay there, for Herod is going to search for the Child to kill Him. 2:13

16. Herod realizes the Magi have tricked him and slaughters all the boys in Bethlehem and the surrounding area who are two years old or under. 2:16

17. Herod dies. 2:19

18. An angel of the Lord appears in a dream to Joseph in Egypt and tells him to return to Israel. "Those who sought the Child's life are dead." 2:19-20

19. Joseph journeys into Israel with Mary and the Child. 2:21

20. Joseph discovers that Archelaus is reigning over Judea and is afraid to go there. 2:22

21. God warns Joseph in a dream, and they leave for the "regions of Galilee." 2:22-23

22. Joseph and Mary settle in a city called Nazareth. 2:2

Luke's* Events At-A-Glance

1. An old priest, Zechariah, is serving in the temple. 1:5-8.   (*verses are NASB version)

2. The angel Gabriel appears to Zechariah and says that Zechariah will have a son and to name him John. 1:11-13

3. When the priest doesn't believe Gabriel, the angel strikes him mute until John is born. 1:18-20

4. Zechariah's wife, Elizabeth, hides her pregnancy for five months. 1:24

5. The next month, the angel Gabriel appears to Mary in Nazareth, a betrothed virgin, and tells her twice that she is favored by God and that she will give birth to a Son by the Holy Spirit and to name Him Jesus. 1:26-35

6. Gabriel also tells Mary that her old relative, Elizabeth, is now six months pregnant. 1:36

7. Mary hurries from Nazareth to the hill country of Judea to Elizabeth and Zechariah's home. 1:39-40

8. When Elizabeth sees Mary, Elizabeth's baby leaps in her womb, and Elizabeth is filled with the Holy Spirit and says, "Blessed are you among women, and blessed is the fruit of your womb! And how has it happened to me that the mother of my Lord would come to me?" 1:41-43

9. Mary then rejoices, saying, "My soul exalts the Lord . . . for the Mighty One has done great things for me . . ." 1:46-55

10. Mary stays with her for roughly three months and then returns to Nazareth. 1:56

11. John is born, Zechariah can suddenly speak, and this frightens his neighbors. All the people in the hill country wonder who John will be. 1:57-66

12. Zechariah prophesies about his son and the Savior. 1:67-79

13. Caesar Augustus orders a census to be taken of all the Roman Empire. 2:1

14. Joseph goes from Nazareth to Bethlehem, because he was of the house of David, to register with Mary. 2:2-5

15. Jesus is born and placed in a manger because there is no room for them. 2:6

16. During the night, in the Bethlehem region, shepherds watching their flocks are met by an angel who tells them the Savior has been born in the city of David. And then an army of angels appears. 2:8-14

17. The shepherds find Jesus. 2:15-16

18. The shepherds make known what was told them about the baby and all are amazed. 2:17

19. Eight days later, Jesus is circumcised and given His name. 2:21

20. When their purification was completed, they brought Jesus to the temple in Jerusalem to present Him to the Lord and to sacrifice. 2:22-24

21. Jesus is blessed in the temple by an elderly man brought there by the Holy Spirit. 2:25-28

22 Jesus is met in the temple by an old prophetess. 2:36-38

<<<---------WHERE ARE THE MAGI, THE SLAUGHTER, & THE FLIGHT TO EGYPT?

23. Joseph and Mary return with their Baby to Nazareth. 2:39

**Brief
At-A-Glance
Combined Timeline**

1. The Genealogy of Jesus - Matthew 1:1-17
Matthew begins his Christmas story with what he feels is most important—the genealogy of Christ.

2. A Greeting to Theophilus - Luke 1:1-4
Luke begins his Christmas account with a greeting. It's an essential part of his Gospel. Luke writes a bright and breezy Christmas story, unlike Matthew's. The greeting unlocks the mystery as to why Luke held back, omitting dark details.

3. Gabriel Announces John the Baptist - Luke 1:5-25
Fifteen months before the birth of Jesus, the angel Gabriel visits the priest Zechariah, telling the old man that he will father a son, John the Baptist.

4. Gabriel Visits Mary - Luke 1:26-38
Six months after Gabriel speaks to Zechariah, the angel is sent to the Virgin Mary to tell her of the upcoming birth of Jesus.

5. Mary Lives with Her Relatives for Three Months - Luke 1:39-56
After Gabriel visits Mary, she travels from Galilee to Judea and stays with Zechariah and his wife for three months.

6. Zechariah Prophesies After the Birth of John - Luke 1:57-80
When John the Baptist is born, Zechariah prophesies about the birth of Jesus.

7. Joseph Learns Mary is with Child - Matthew 1:18-25
When Mary returns to Nazareth, she is three months pregnant. At

some point, Joseph learns of Mary's pregnancy, and an angel tells Joseph in a dream to take Mary as his wife.

8. Caesar Augustus Orders a Roman Census - Luke 2:1-3

Luke, the historian, continues his Christmas story by telling of the decree by Caesar Augustus that all the inhabitants of Rome should return to their towns to be counted.

9. Jesus is Born in Bethlehem - Luke 2:4-20

Jesus is born, and the Christmas Angel tells the news to shepherds, who then find the Baby in a manger in Bethlehem.

10. Jesus is Circumcised and Presented - Luke 2:21-40

Jesus is taken to the temple when He is eight days old to be named and circumcised. Jesus is there again when He is 40 days old to fulfill the Law of Moses.

11. The Magi Arrive and the Flight to Egypt - Matthew 2:1-18

Arguably, the Magi then arrive in Jerusalem after seeing the star for the King of the Jews. Herod learns the time of the star's rising and sends them to Bethlehem once he's advised that this is where prophecy expects the Messiah to be born.

The Magi follow the star and present gifts to Jesus, but they are warned not to return to Herod and leave by another route. Joseph is warned in a dream to flee because Herod is going to kill the Child.

12. The Death of Herod and Return to Nazareth - Matthew 2:19-23

After Joseph flees to Egypt with Mary and Jesus, the massacre of the children occurs, and then, at some point, Herod dies.

Joseph returns to Israel with his family after being told to do so by an angel, and then God tells him to go to Nazareth.

Note: Luke also says the family returned to Nazareth in No. 10 above, but Luke does not include the Magi, the massacre, or the flight to Egypt. Luke may have had a very good reason, which we'll examine.

At-A-Glance
Combined Timeline
with Verses

The Genealogy

1. The genealogy of Jesus. (Mt. 1:1-17)

Gabriel Announces John the Baptist

1. An old priest, Zechariah, is serving in the temple. (Lk. 1:5-8)

2. The angel Gabriel appears to Zechariah and says that Zechariah will have a son and to name him John. (Lk. 1:11-13)

3. When the priest doesn't believe Gabriel, the angel strikes him mute until John is born. (Lk. 1:18-20)

4. Zechariah's wife, Elizabeth, hides her pregnancy for five months. (Lk. 1:24)

Gabriel Visits Mary

1. The next month, the angel Gabriel appears to Mary in Nazareth, a betrothed virgin, and tells her twice that she is favored by God and that she will give birth to a Son by the Holy Spirit and to name him Jesus. (Lk. 1:26-35)

2. Gabriel also tells Mary that her old relative, Elizabeth, is now six months pregnant. (Lk. 1:36)

Mary Is with Her Relatives for Three Months, Rejoicing

1. Mary hurries from Nazareth to the hill country of Judea to Elizabeth and Zechariah's home. (Lk. 1:39-40)

2. When Elizabeth sees Mary, Elizabeth's baby leaps in her womb, and Elizabeth is filled with the Holy Spirit and says, "Blessed are you among women, and blessed is the fruit of your womb! And how has it happened to me that the mother of my Lord would come to me?" (Lk. 1:41-43)

3. Mary then rejoices, saying, "My soul exalts the Lord . . . for the Mighty One has done great things for me . . ." (Lk. 1:46-55)

4. Mary stays with her for roughly three months and then returns to Nazareth. (Lk. 1:56)

Zechariah Prophesies After the Birth of John

1. John is born and Zechariah can suddenly speak, which frightens his neighbors. All the people in the hill country wonder who John will be. (Lk. 1:57-66)

2. Zechariah prophesies about his son and the Savior. (Lk. 1:67-79)

Joseph Learns Mary is with Child

1. The Virgin Mary, betrothed to Joseph, is found to be pregnant by the Holy Spirit. (Mt. 1:18)

. . .

LOVE

2. Joseph plans to send Mary away secretly so she won't be disgraced. (Mt. 1:19)

3. In a dream, an angel of the Lord tells Joseph that the Child was conceived by the Holy Spirit. (Mt. 1:20)

4. Joseph is told to name him Jesus for he will save his people from their sins. (Mt. 1:21)

5. Joseph awakes and does as the angel of the Lord commanded and takes Mary as his wife. (Mt. 1:24)

Caesar Augustus Orders a Roman Census

1. Caesar Augustus orders a census be taken of all the Roman Empire. (Lk. 2:1)

2. Joseph goes from Nazareth to Bethlehem, because he was of the house of David, to register with Mary. (Lk. 2:2-5)

Jesus is Born in Bethlehem

1. Jesus is born in Bethlehem of Judea in the days of Herod the King. (Mt. 1:25-2:1)

2. Jesus is born and placed in a manger because there is no room for them. (Lk. 2:6)

. . .

3. During the night in the Bethlehem region, shepherds watching their flocks are met by an angel who tells them the Savior has been born in the city of David. And then an army of angels appears. (Lk. 2:8-14)

4. The shepherds find Jesus. (Lk. 2:15-16)

5. The shepherds make known what was told them about the baby, and all are amazed. (Lk. 2:17)

Jesus is Circumcised and Presented

1. Eight days after His birth, Jesus is circumcised and given His name. (Lk. 2:21)

2. When their purification was completed, they brought Jesus to the temple in Jerusalem to present Him to the Lord and sacrifice. This was a time of cleansing for Mary, 40 days after Jesus's birth. (Lk. 2:22-24)

3. Mary and Joseph appear to offer a sacrifice according to the Law of Moses: "A pair of turtledoves or two young doves." (Lk. 2:24)

4. Jesus is blessed in the temple by an elderly man brought there by the Holy Spirit. (Lk. 2:25-28)

5 Jesus is met in the temple by an old prophetess. (Lk. 2:36-38)

The Magi Arrive and the Subsequent Flight to Egypt

LOVE

1. Magi arrive, asking where the King of the Jews was born, that they saw his star in the East and have come to worship him. (Mt. 2:1-2)

2. Herod is troubled, and all of Jerusalem is troubled. (Mt. 2:3)

3. Herod gathers the chief priests and scribes to learn where the Messiah was to be born, and they say Bethlehem. (Mt. 2:4-6)

4. Herod secretly meets with the magi to determine the exact time the star appeared. (Mt. 2:7)

5. Herod sends the magi to Bethlehem..." telling them to report after they find Him. (Mt. 2:8)

6. The magi leave Jerusalem, the star goes ahead of them, and stops where the Child is. (Mt. 2:9)

7. The magi are warned in a dream not to return to Herod and leave for their country a different way. (Mt. 2:12)

8. After the magi are gone, an angel of the Lord appears to Joseph in a dream and says to get up and flee to Egypt and stay there until I tell you, for Herod is going to search for the Child to kill Him. (Mt. 2:13)

9. Herod realizes the magi have tricked him, and he slaughters all the boys in Bethlehem and the surrounding area who are two years old or under. (Mt. 2:16)

The Death of Herod and the Return from Egypt

1. Herod dies. (Mt. 2:19)

2. In a dream, an angel of the Lord tells Joseph in Egypt to return to Israel for "those who sought the Child's life are dead." (Mt. 2:19-20)

3. Joseph journeys into Israel with Mary and the Child. (Mt. 2:21)

4. Joseph discovers that Archelaus is reigning over Judea and is afraid to go there. (Mt. 2:22)

5. God warns Joseph in a dream, and they leave for the "regions of Galilee." (Mt. 2:22-23)

Nazareth

1. Joseph and Mary settle in a city called Nazareth. (Mt. 2:2)

2. Joseph and Mary return with their baby to Nazareth. (Lk. 2:39)

All verses are from the NASB

Keep These Points in Mind

1. Luke leaves the Magi out entirely.

2. Matthew omits the two trips to the Jerusalem temple. Both were important to comply with the Law of Moses, and they happened on certain days:

Mary & Joseph presented Jesus at the temple when he was eight days old to be named and circumcised. They also returned to the temple for their purification, which was 40 days after Jesus's birth. They offered birds, the sacrifice of the poor.

3. If the Magi had already arrived, bringing great wealth, Mary and Joseph could have offered a lamb.

4. Thus, it's likely the Magi arrived after Jesus was 40 days old.

5. Also remember that the family could not have been in Egypt when Jesus was eight days old and forty days old and taken to the temple. So, again, it's most likely the Magi came after Jesus was 40 days old.

Notes, Revelations, Prayers

Date:_____

3. THE GREATEST GIFT

THE GIFT YOU MUST HAVE THIS CHRISTMAS

"The Spirit Himself intercedes for us with groanings too deep for words."

Romans 8:26[1]

---

1. ESV

THE GIFT YOU MUST HAVE THIS CHRISTMAS

It was a bitterly cold winter night. I didn't care. I'd had a really discouraging day and wanted to go for a long drive.

This was December of 2020, the first year of the coronavirus for the United States.

When I stopped at a streetlight in a nearby city, I saw a young man sitting on the sidewalk. He didn't have a sign seeking help. He just sat there.

"Are you hungry?" I asked, rolling down my window. "If I get you something, will you eat it?"

He didn't say anything, and I thought he couldn't hear me.

I asked again.

I had stopped on what was usually a busy artery, but it was nearly midnight and there was no traffic. I waited as he remained seated on that cold sidewalk.

Finally, he nodded.

Minutes later, I returned with hot chili and a sandwich, uncertain as to how I would give it to him. I'm careful with homeless people I don't know.

He was gone.

I looked everywhere, but he had disappeared.

That's when I noticed a little old man with a homeless sign on a different corner. Had he been there before? I hadn't seen him.

I turned into a gas station across from him, opened my car door, and set the bags out on the street corner. Customers pumping fuel eyed me—confused. They hadn't seen him standing on the other side of that three-lane boulevard.

But the old man knew what was what.

Before I could call to him, he had started across the street, and I quickly closed my door. As I said, I'm careful. That's why I set the food on the corner.

Then I exited the other side of the gas station and went on my way.

I hadn't planned on doing anything for anybody that night—I was so filled with my own pain. But the bitterly freezing weather moved me. A person willing to brave that kind of cold must have been hungry.

As I drove away, the darkness inside me lifted, replaced with Light and happiness. My mom had died years before, but I thought of her. She told me that my grandmother would never turn away from any hungry person. And she taught me to do the same.

Those are great memories—being with my mom and feeding people like him.

Don't misunderstand me. That year, 2020, was terribly hard, and people had nothing to give. Even wealthy people, usually insulated from crisis, were beleaguered. They didn't escape the rampage of the coronavirus. We all knew someone who had been hospitalized or died.

And the struggle continues with a rough economy now in 2024.

So, I am not suggesting that you should add anything to the burden that you carry. Don't offer a random act of kindness just to get it done.

Instead, I am saying this—expect the Holy Spirit.

If you are afraid, or sad, or overwhelmed, know this: God is with you. Expect the Spirit to lead you down a road to a moment in time that you need.

I wasn't at the street corner for the old man. I was there for me.

I went for that long drive because I needed to be with God. I have decisions to make, and they overwhelm me.

Scripture says, "The Spirit helps us in our weakness. For we do not

LOVE

know what to pray for as we ought, but the Spirit Himself intercedes for us with groanings too deep for words."[1]

It's one of the most beautiful passages in Scripture.

Christmas comes this year to millions discouraged by the events of the past four years. We all face the unknown in this divided nation.

It's become an angry age.

What you may not realize is that Jesus was born into an angrier time. The political climate was far worse than what we've seen—Herod had lost power and, upon his return, murdered countless people. He was bent on revenge.

Understand that this is why no one in Jerusalem rejoiced when news arrived about Jesus, a new king. The thought of a political turnover was daunting. You may have overlooked this passage because it's hard to believe any first-century Jew winced at the arrival of the Messiah. But that was true in Jerusalem. Here it is:

"Now after Jesus was born in Bethlehem of Judea in the days of Herod the king, behold, magi from the east arrived in Jerusalem, saying, 'Where is He who has been born King of the Jews? For we saw His star in the east and have come to worship Him.' When Herod the king heard this, he was troubled, and **all Jerusalem with him.**"[2]

We are rarely told of the civil wars in Rome in the first century B.C. before Jesus was born. Herod allied himself with Marc Antony and Cleopatra, the losing side, in one of the most important of these wars. In the midst of the turmoil, another nation seized Jerusalem in bloody warfare, and that brought the death[3] of Herod's brother.

I am a theologian, not a historian.[4] But I will do my best to show you in this *Christmas Edition* of *Reaching to God* what happened, so you can understand why all of Jerusalem was upset—no one wanted more bloodshed. The turmoil also explains why Herod murdered the

---

1. Romans 8:26, ESV
2. Matthew 2:1-3, NASB, emphasis added
3. I have read that he was tortured and committed suicide, and also that he was murdered by the Parthians.
4. There isn't a lot written about Herod and the Roman Civil Wars. Perhaps a historian will step forward and clarify this period for Christians. I've made the invitation.

children in Bethlehem and the vicinity. Rome had given Herod the title "King of the Jews." No one was taking it from him.

Those in Jerusalem, in their fear, did not realize that God had decided to hand out the best gift a person can have. Jesus.

It was Christmas!

Returning home that cold night, I passed near the corner where I had left the food for the little old man.

But remember the young man? The one sitting on the corner with no sign? I spotted him again. Somehow.

I say that because he had found a place almost completely hidden from traffic. Clearly, he hadn't wanted my food. What he wanted was to be left alone.

Perhaps what he longed for that bitterly cold night was the same thing I needed—to be with God.

"Come unto me all ye that labour and are heavy laden and I will give you rest."[5]

However you celebrate Christmas this year, remember God's gift to you: Jesus, the Son of God.

You do not face the future alone. The Lord is always present with you. Turn to Him.

Jesus is your comfort and strength.[6]

---

5. Matthew 11:28, KJV
6. The *Palm Beach Post*, and additional newspapers across the nation, published this Christmas message on December 25, 2020.

Notes, Revelations, Prayers

Date:_____

4. WHEREVER YOU GO

HE LIVED A LIFE OF ADVENTURE

"Fear not, for I am with you; Be not dismayed, for I am your God."

Isaiah 41:10[1]

---

1. NKJV

HE LIVED A LIFE OF ADVENTURE

The man lived a life of adventure. When you hear his story, you may not see it that way. Not at first.

The drama began with his beloved. The man had solid proof that his girlfriend, actually his fiancée, had been with someone else. Even so, he decided to marry her. The child wasn't his, but he loved the boy.

Immediately, this new father started to notice strange things—unknown visitors showed up at his door. It didn't happen once but repeatedly. Some of these people were dirty laborers and others very wealthy.

Why? He didn't know.

But the situation got far worse.

One night, as he was sleeping, this new father had a nightmare. In the dream, he was told a raid was planned for his home.

This wasn't a government agency—not the IRS, coming the next afternoon with a search warrant for his tax records. Special Forces was about to descend on this man's house, drag the new baby boy from his bed, and murder the child.

Upon awaking, did this man turn over and go back to sleep? Did he get up and take a walk in the night, trying to clear his head? Did he discuss the dream in the morning with a trusted friend?

No.

The man quickly grabbed his family. They fled in the dark of night, hurrying until they crossed the border to safety in a neighboring land.

I wrote this column for the Northwest Florida Daily News and a series of other newspapers at the end of 2018. I distinctly remember that night. I was overwhelmed with fear. God had made it clear that I had to go—leave my home and travel nearly 1,000 miles away.

But why?

Where had I gone wrong?

I had nowhere safe to go. What was going to become of me?

I reached for my Bible and it fell open to this story. I suddenly realized how traumatic these true events were. The man is Joseph, the father of baby Jesus.

Joseph must have been quite happy at the outset. He'd snagged the best girl, by far—Gabriel tells us Mary had found favor with God.[1]

But Joseph's joy was short-lived, soon discovering she was with child. Definitely not what he'd expected.

Clearly, Joseph was close to God. Altogether, he had four dreams, with an angel appearing in three to guide him.

The first dream occurred as Joseph considered divorcing Mary. In our way of thinking, they were not yet married, but in that culture, she was betrothed and legally considered married. The arrangement was fixed and would have required a divorce.

"Joseph, son of David," an angel said. "Do not fear to take Mary as your wife, for that which is conceived in her is from the Holy Spirit."[2]

Joseph awakened and knew his future—he was getting married.[3]

Upon the birth of his baby, and I mean on day one, strangers showed up. Probably surprised young shepherds, gawking. And, later, very wealthy visitors from faraway lands. They arrived with expensive gifts.

Moreover, the Wise Men knelt to worship Joseph's child.

---

1. Luke 1:30
2. Matthew 1:20, ESV
3. Matthew 1:24-25

LOVE

Unsettling—to say the least.

And then the second dream, which led to the night of terror. "Rise," an angel said. "Take the child and His mother and flee to Egypt . . . for Herod is about to search for the child to destroy Him."[4]

Joseph didn't hesitate.

He didn't go back to sleep, didn't go for a walk, didn't talk it over with anyone. Joseph got up, grabbed his family, and raced from the city in darkness, running to the border.

Then, upon the death of Herod the Great, there was a third dream. "Rise . . . and go to the land of Israel," an angel said, "for those who sought the child's life are dead."[5]

In the fourth dream, God warned Joseph to take his family north to Nazareth to escape Herod's son.

Looking at Joseph on my fearful night years ago, I saw his life as I never had. The virgin birth, the strange visitors, the night of panic, life as a fugitive, and the dangerous return.

As I finish writing this Christmas book in 2024, it's dark outside. I'm sitting exactly where I was six years ago, having returned two years ago from my time away. Tears glaze my eyes as I remember that night—facing a frightening future.

Clearly, Joseph's life was upended.

For how long? We don't know. What we do know is that, although he faced crisis after crisis, he kept moving forward. Here's why:

Joseph had made peace with his future—he knew wherever he went, whatever happened, the Lord would be there. Joseph had lived his life alongside God, and Joseph trusted Him.

That was my answer to my fear six years ago. Move forward. God, who had always been with me, wasn't going to leave me now.

As I headed out on my trip, a friend called me. When I told him where I was going, he said, "Where will you stay?"

Once he realized my situation, he made another call. Moments

---

4. Matthew 2:13
5. Matthew 2:20

later, he was back on the phone. His mother, whom I hardly knew, opened her home to me.

You may be facing trouble, worried for yourself or your family. Your situation may feel overwhelming. You may be suffering—unable to sleep, eating too much or too little.

Listen to me. Draw close to God: Sing a hymn, pray, meditate (there are plenty of online meditation videos), reach for your Bible. Let it fall open as I did on that awful December night.

God will speak to you.

As surely as the Lord guided Joseph, He will guide you.

You can look at your life as an adventure, knowing this one thing—whatever happens, you do not walk alone. God is with you.

Notes, Revelations, Prayers

Date:_____

JOY

"[They] were overjoyed when they saw the Lord."

John 20:20[1]

---

1. NIV

JOY TO THE WORLD
THE LORD HAS COME

5. MARY AND ELIZABETH

TWO WOMEN WHO CELEBRATE BEFORE CHRISTMAS

"…nothing is impossible with God."

Luke 1:37[1]

---

1. NLT

TWO WOMEN WHO CELEBRATE BEFORE CHRISTMAS

As a rule of thumb, you don't want to make an angel mad. But he did just that. And, honestly, it was so unlike this old priest. The Bible describes him as "righteous before God, walking blamelessly in all the commandments and statutes of the Lord."[1]

So what went wrong?

It seems the old man had his heart set on having a child before he died. He had prayed earnestly to God year after year. Then, suddenly, an angel appeared to him in the temple and said, "Do not be afraid, Zechariah, for your prayer has been heard."[2]

The angel said his old, barren wife would give birth to a son and to name him John. "And he will . . . make ready for the Lord a people prepared."[3]

That's when the trouble began—the holy man didn't believe the angel. And it gets worse. This was not your run-of-the-mill heavenly host.

"I am Gabriel," the angel announced. Can't you see him arching to

---

1. Luke 1:6, ESV
2. Luke 1:13, ESV
3. Luke 1:16-17, ESV

his full height, spreading his massive wings as far as they would go?[4] "I stand in the presence of God."[5]

Oooooh. See what I mean?

Listen closely and you can hear his words echoing off the gold and marble of the temple. This old priest needed to know with whom he was dealing.

And here it comes.

"Behold, you will be silent," Gabriel announced. "Unable to speak until the day these things take place, because you did not believe my words . . ."[6]

Gabriel left and six months later the angel was given one of the highest honors in heaven: Gabriel was sent with a message for a virgin.

"In the sixth month the angel Gabriel was sent from God to a city in Galilee named Nazareth, to a virgin betrothed to a man whose name was Joseph . . . and the virgin's name was Mary. And coming in, he said to her, 'Greetings, favored one! The Lord is with you.'

"But she was very perplexed at this statement, and was pondering what kind of greeting this was.

"And the angel said to her, 'Do not be afraid, Mary, for you have found favor with God.

"'And behold, you will conceive in your womb and give birth to a son, and you shall name Him Jesus. He will . . . be called the Son of the Most High; and . . . His kingdom will have no end.'

"But Mary said to the angel, 'How will this be, since I am a virgin?'

"The angel answered and said to her, 'The Holy Spirit will come upon you, and the power of the Most High will overshadow you; for that reason also the holy Child will be called the Son of God.

"'And behold, even your relative Elizabeth herself has conceived a

---

4. Full disclosure: Gabriel may or may not have had wings. Sometimes angels appear as ordinary men but at other times their appearance creates fear. This was one of the fearful times. It would seem that he did not look simply like a man, hence my reference to the wings. We know from the Ark of the Covenant that the cherubim had very large wings.
5. Luke 1:19, ESV
6. Luke 1:20, ESV

son in her old age, and she who was called infertile is now in her sixth month.'"[7]

This second passage, when Gabriel came to Mary, begins by saying Gabriel came in the sixth month. "In the sixth month the angel Gabriel was sent from God to a city in Galilee named Nazareth, to a virgin . . ."

It was now six months after Gabriel had appeared to Zechariah. And the sixth month of Elizabeth's pregnancy.

Unlike Zechariah's doubt, look at Mary's final words to Gabriel. Mary said, "May it be done to me according to your word."[8]

Many think when Mary learned she would give birth by the Holy Spirit that she was afraid and kept quiet, only telling Joseph, to whom she was engaged.

Not so. Look at how the passage continues:

"Now at this time, Mary set out and went in a hurry to the hill country, to a city of Judah, and she entered the house of Zechariah and greeted Elizabeth."[9]

When Mary stepped inside the old woman's home, Scripture says the woman shouted, "Blessed are you among women, and blessed is the fruit of your womb!"[10]

This was Mary's cousin, Elizabeth. Obviously, the relative knew Mary was carrying the Messiah. Scripture says the old woman's words burst forth, coming from the Holy Spirit.

Elizabeth said, "And how has it happened to me that the mother of my Lord would come to me?"[11]

If you give that some thought, it's an amazing moment. This old woman and young virgin are similarly situated.

How so?

One was too old to give birth, yet six months pregnant. The other was a virgin but also with child.

The impossible made possible!

---

7. Luke 1:26-36, NASB
8. Luke 1:38, NASB
9. Luke 1:39-40, NASB
10. Luke 1:42, NASB
11. Luke 1:42, NASB

Mary stayed with her cousins, Elizabeth and, yes, old Zechariah, until their child arrived. Here's the passage:

"Mary stayed with her about three months, and then returned to her home."[12]

Six months later, Jesus was born.

Many believe this was a fearful time for Mary. Not so. Look at the Biblical accounts of those months. Luke paints a vivid picture of Mary celebrating. He writes of her singing, "My soul exalts the Lord . . . the Mighty One has done great things for me . . ."[13]

I placed all of her song of praise, which is called "The Magnificat," at the end of this chapter. Magnificat in Latin means "my soul magnifies the Lord."

And why not celebrate? Both women now know the outcome of the prophecies hundreds of years old:

"A voice cries, 'In the wilderness, prepare the way of the LORD; make straight in the desert a highway for our God.'" (Isaiah 40:3)[14]

"Behold, the virgin shall conceive and bear a son, and shall call his name Immanuel." (Isaiah 7:14)[15]

Both Mary and Elizabeth could see Isaiah's prophecies unfolding.

The first prophecy:

"A voice cries, 'In the wilderness, prepare the way of the LORD; make straight in the desert a highway for our God.'"

This was the foretelling of John the Baptist, who was in Elizabeth's womb. John the Baptist was born to prepare the way of the Lord.

And the second prophecy:

"Behold, the virgin shall conceive and bear a son, and shall call his name Immanuel."

That virgin was Mary, who was carrying Jesus.

Those two women now knew that those ancient words were about them! We can't begin to know how they felt.

Mary and Elizabeth also knew when the hoped-for promises would

---

12. Luke 1:56, NASB
13. Luke 1:46-49, NASB
14. ESV
15. ESV

occur. The exact time. Each could count the *months* until the prophecies would be fulfilled!

They could also see the very place Isaiah's words would come to pass. For John the Baptist, the prophet would be born right there in Elizabeth's home. For the Messiah, Jesus would be born six months later in Israel.

It's an exciting time!

Can't you see the two cooking and singing, dancing and praising God, chatting joyously?

But, wait. Are we forgetting someone?

There's a third figure in the story Luke sets forth.

Zechariah.

In the midst of the women's joy, there was poor old Zechariah, who couldn't utter a peep. Why? Because he doubted Gabriel. Because he did not trust God.

Don't make that same mistake. Believe!

When you earnestly pray, believe! Listen to the final words Gabriel spoke to Mary. Memorize them.

"…nothing is impossible with God."[16]

---

16. Luke 1:37, NLT

Reflection

I wrote this chapter at Christmas in 2016 for my newspaper column. I remember a prominent man in my church approaching me that Sunday, beaming.

"I didn't realize Mary was so happy!" he said. "I never saw that!"

In fact, everyone I knew believed that Mary was alone and afraid upon discovering that she was with Child.

I also had been taught this, perhaps because it seems logical or because the Gospel of Matthew is first to tell the Christmas story, and Matthew definitely leaves you with that impression. Look at his words:

"Now the birth of Jesus the Messiah was as follows: when His mother Mary had been betrothed to Joseph, before they came together she was found to be pregnant by the Holy Spirit. And her husband Joseph, since he was a righteous man and did not want to disgrace her, planned to send her away secretly."[1]

It seems like a sad scene, but only if you look at Matthew's words without adding Luke's. As you just saw, Mary wasn't sitting home worrying what the neighbors would think. She was very happy!

In 2017, the next year, the first book in the *Reaching to God* series was published, and it begins with this chapter. That's because Mary and Elizabeth will always be a favorite!

By that time, I had been a columnist for two years and had written over 100 columns[2], but this one was special. It isn't just that Mary was so happy or that those two 700-year-old prophecies were fulfilled.

It's because the elderly woman and the virgin girl were the same!

Don't miss that—God made this decision *deliberately*. One too old to give birth yet six months pregnant, and the other a virgin but also with child. Two impossibles made possible.

We have a splendid God, and this was His moment to shine!

---

1. Matthew 1:18-19, NASB
2. A newspaper "column" is essentially just a recurring article written by the same person, the columnist. It derives from the physical vertical column of text in the newspaper.

MARY'S WORDS OF CELEBRATION
The Magnificat
Luke 1:46-55[1]

And Mary said: "My soul exalts the Lord,
And my spirit has rejoiced in God my Savior.

For He has had regard for the humble state of His bond-servant;
For behold, from now on all generations will call me blessed.
For the Mighty One has done great things for me;
And holy is His name.

And His mercy is to generation after generation
Toward those who fear Him.
He has done mighty deeds with His arm;
He has scattered those who were proud
in the thoughts of their hearts.

He has brought down rulers from their thrones,
And has exalted those who were humble.
He has filled the hungry with good things,
And sent the rich away empty-handed.

He has given help to His servant Israel,
In remembrance of His mercy,
Just as He spoke to our fathers,
To Abraham and his descendants forever."

---

1. NASB

Notes, Revelations, Prayers

Date:_____

6. CAESAR AUGUSTUS

GOD GOES BIG FOR HIS SON'S BIRTHDAY

"Now in those days a decree went out from Caesar Augustus that a census be taken of all the inhabited earth."

Luke 2:1[1]

---

1. NASB

GOD GOES BIG FOR HIS SON'S BIRTHDAY

Setting the Historical Stage

It's the most ordinary of things for historians to do—linking major world events to those in power.
1. Pearl Harbor – FDR
2. The Bombing of Britain – Winston Churchill
3. The Korean War – Harry Truman
4. The Cuban Missile Crisis - John F. Kennedy
5. Watergate - Richard Nixon

Scripture does this as well.

Luke is perhaps the finest historian of all time. I added a chapter on Josephus after this one for those who have read objections to Luke's account.

Luke wrote over a quarter of the New Testament, and his writings are different from the others, as you will see.

Look at Chapter 3 of Luke's Gospel. Although this passage occurs long after the Christmas story, it's important because you see how Luke introduces John the Baptist to his readers, tying that moment to those in power:

"In the fifteenth year of the reign of Tiberius Caesar, Pontius Pilate being governor of Judea, and Herod[1] being tetrarch of Galilee, and his brother Philip tetrarch of the region of Ituraea and Trachonitis, and Lysanias tetrarch of Abilene, during the high priesthood of Annas and Caiaphas, the word of God came to John the son of Zechariah in the wilderness."[2]

Sounds like ordinary historian information—linking events to those in power.

Watch as Luke does the same thing with the birth of Christ, placing that moment on the historical stage, telling us who was reigning at that time.

"In those days a decree went out from Caesar Augustus that all the world should be registered. This was the first registration when [or this was the registration before][3] Quirinius was governor of Syria. And all went to be registered, each to his own town. And Joseph also went up from Galilee, from the town of Nazareth, to Judea, to the city of David, which is called Bethlehem, because he was of the house and lineage of David, to be registered with Mary, his betrothed, who was with child."[4]

Typical historian behavior, anchoring the birth of Jesus in history.

Right?

At first glance, it appears so, but there's much more here—those verses are BIG. The passage is incredibly exciting!

Let me show you. We need to look at two important points.

The Prophecy

First, some 700 years before the birth of Christ, the prophet Micah spoke these words from God:

"But as for you, Bethlehem Ephrathah,
Too little to be among the clans of Judah,
From you One will come forth for Me to be ruler in Israel.
His times of coming forth are from long ago,

---

1. Remember that Herod the Great is dead. This is his son.
2. Luke 3:1-2, ESV
3. It can be interpreted both ways.
4. Luke 2:1-5, ESV

From the days of eternity."[5]

Micah prophesied that the Messiah would be born in Bethlehem.

Where Was Mary?

The second point we need to look at is that Joseph took Mary to be registered. But where was Mary?

Remember, the angel Gabriel told her she would bear the Son of God, and Mary then went to see Elizabeth. We just read that passage in the chapter "Mary and Elizabeth." But where is she now?

1. Nazareth
2. Galilee
3. Some 80 miles north of Bethlehem
4. All of the above
5. None of the above

Look over your choices carefully and then decide. The answer is in the three passages we just studied with the help of a map:

First: "…the angel Gabriel was sent from God to a city in Galilee named Nazareth, to a virgin."[6]

Second: "Now at this time, Mary set out and went in a hurry to the hill country, to a city of Judah, and she entered the house of Zechariah and greeted Elizabeth."[7]

Third: "Mary stayed with her about three months, and then returned to her home."[8]

So, Scripture tells us Gabriel came to Mary in Nazareth in Galilee, then Mary went away for three months, and then she returned to Nazareth, which is some 80 miles north of Bethlehem. The answer is No. 4, "All of the above." See the map on the next pages.

I encourage you to look at a map frequently as you study Scripture, otherwise you won't see important information as occurs here.

Do you see the logistical problem?

---

5. Micah 5:2, NASB
6. Luke 1:26, NASB
7. Luke 1:39-40, NASB
8. Luke 1:56, NASB

First Century AD Map

Mediterranean Sea

GALILEE Sea of Galilee

Nazareth

Jordan River

SAMARIA

JUDEA Jerusalem

Bethlehem

Dead Sea

The Logistics

God knew that Mary had to give birth in Bethlehem to fulfill the Christmas prophecy. That's why I say this is so exciting.

How did God get Mary from Nazareth in Galilee to Bethlehem in Judea, where she needed to be? She was 80 miles north.

He could have easily sent Gabriel to tell Joseph and Mary to visit Joseph's family in Bethlehem. That would have worked.

Or Mary and Joseph could have been passing through Bethlehem on their way to Jerusalem. Or they could have been farther south for some reason, traveling north, and then they could have stopped in Bethlehem.

Clearly, the trip to fulfill prophecy could have happened in any number of humdrum ways.

But, no.

Not for the birth of the Son of God!

The Timing

The Roman Empire was huge, and travel was not easy. Scripture doesn't tell us when the decree was issued or how much time each person had to fulfill the commitment, but we do know Mary was nine months pregnant and gave birth in Bethlehem.

In other words, did Joseph put off this trip, hoping she would give birth before they had to leave? The long trip would have been very hard on her. And then did he finally have no choice but to leave to meet the deadline?

Or maybe Caesar didn't give his inhabitants time to plan, instead ordering them to go, and they went. This seems more likely.

We don't know, but whatever happened, the fact that she was so very pregnant is interesting. It was also necessary. Otherwise, they could have registered, left, and Jesus would have been born elsewhere.

Mary needed to be nine months pregnant when they arrived.

Joy

Caesar's Decree

Look also at Caesar's census.

God could have led Caesar Augustus to direct the decree only at the Jews. That would have worked to fulfill prophecy, because God just needed to make sure Mary was in Bethlehem when she gave birth.

But, no. Not for the birth of His Son. God went all in, moving countless subjects of Rome!

Here's the passage:

"Now in those days a decree went out from Caesar Augustus, that a census be taken of all the inhabited earth.[1] This was the first census taken[2] while Quirinius[3] was governor of Syria. And all the people were on their way to register for the census, each to his own city.

"Now Joseph also went up from Galilee, from the city of Nazareth, to Judea, to the city of David which is called Bethlehem, because he was of the house and family of David, in order to register along with Mary, who was betrothed to him, and was pregnant."[4]

That decree went out to perhaps 45 million people.[5]

On the next pages, you can see just how big the Roman Empire was under Caesar Augustus.[6] Mary and Joseph probably passed countless subjects of Rome as they traveled south to Bethlehem.

Listen to me, it wasn't a simple coincidence that Caesar's decree was in effect when Mary was both nine months pregnant and in the wrong place.

It also wasn't a mere coincidence that it went to all the inhabitants of the Roman world. God did it deliberately.

His precious Child was about to be born, and God goes BIG—countless Roman subjects had to get up and move!

---

1. This can also be translated as the Roman Empire.
2. It can also be translated: or this took place as a first census
3. Luke has been criticized because of the dating of Quirinius. But archaeologist Sir Ramsay discovered inscriptions that Quirinius was in Syria twice. See the next chapter.
4. Luke 2:1-5, NASB, emphasis added
5. Britannica estimate.
6. Cristiano64, CC BY-SA 3.0 <http://creativecommons.org/licenses/by-sa/3.0/>, via Wikimedia Commons

Tonight, look up at the stars. The Lord is capable of anything.

Place your heart in His Hands, and know just how great your powerful, almighty Father is.

Tell Him your needs, believe in His power, and listen for His guidance.

Nothing is too big for Him.

Notes, Revelations, Prayers

Date:_____

7. JOSEPHUS

A THUMB ON THE SCALE

"Do not be deceived: God cannot be mocked.
A man reaps what he sows."

Galatians 6:7[1]

---

1. NIV

A THUMB ON THE SCALE

This is very important.

In 1915, Sir William M. Ramsay published *The Bearing of Recent Discovery on the Trustworthiness of the New Testament*. Ramsay, an archaeologist, explains in his book how he overcame his skepticism about Luke's writings.

Ramsay found Luke to be a first-rate historian!

It's important because you will read that Luke was sloppy. That's because of the writings of the oft-quoted Flavius Josephus, a first-century A.D. "historian."

You'll see in a minute why I put historian in quotes.

Josephus was critical of Luke, but Josephus's writings are wrong. Josephus said Quirinius was governor nearly a decade after Herod's death. This was to discredit Luke's account of how most of Rome moved at the birth of Jesus.

As it turns out, archaeology proves Quirinius was in power twice.

Josephus, a Jew, lived c. 37-100 A.D. and was a contemporary of Luke. So Josephus would have known this as well as Luke.

Did Josephus hide that?

Josephus never knew Jesus. He began writing long after the death and resurrection of Jesus. But the writings of Josephus contain ugly things about the Lord. When I saw those words in Josephus's writings, I gave his books away.

A historian doesn't put his or her thumb on the scale and try to change history. More than one person has seen that in Josephus's writings—he changed data to support his position. For instance, the Britannica says, "His writings are not always accepted as totally reliable."

And yet Josephus is treated far and wide as a careful historian.

If he isn't "totally reliable," what part should be viewed as reliable?

I hear ministers quote him and know that they have no idea what Josephus's writings say about Jesus.

Be careful with Josephus and sources that rely on him. Decide whether to trust conclusions drawn from his writings. If you can't find independent confirmation for what Josephus puts forward, decide whether to believe it.

Remember what I said at the outset. In 1915, the archaeologist Sir William M. Ramsay published *The Bearing of Recent Discovery on the Trustworthiness of the New Testament*.

Based on archaeology, Ramsay said Luke was a first-rate historian!

Josephus, on the other hand, recorded first-century history incorrectly, even though Josephus and Luke were both first century historians.

Josephus was either incredibly confused or he did it deliberately, placing his thumb on the scale, bent on shaping history into what suited his cause. From the whole of it, both his statements about Jesus and Quirinius. one such cause appears to be an effort to discredit and show contempt for Jesus and the Christian faith.

I owe more loyalty to my Lord than to read or rely on the writings of such a man.

Notes, Revelations, Prayers

Date:_____

8. MICAH'S PROPHECY

OH LITTLE TOWN OF BETHLEHEM

"Yes, my soul, find rest in God; my hope comes from Him."

Psalm 62:5[1]

---

1. NIV

OH LITTLE TOWN OF BETHLEHEM

If you live in Florida, you wouldn't have been surprised when U.S. News[1] reported that Florida was the best place in the entire nation for a family vacation.

In the entire nation!

Specifically, Orlando-Walt Disney.

You could have been the guy changing tires at Sam's Club in Fort Walton Beach, Florida, who had never read U.S. News, and still know Florida was the nation's No. 1 vacation spot—boundless sunshine, white-sand beaches, clear emerald water.

But ask an auto parts guy in Buffalo, New York, who's never been to Florida, and he might scratch his head.

On the other hand, if it's December 2024, you better believe that auto parts guy in Buffalo knew the Buffalo Bills quarterback Josh Allen had just been named the NFL's Most Valuable Player, and that the Bills, barring injuries, had a shot at the Super Bowl!

You know why? People take pride in what they have!

The same is true in the Bible.

One little town must have had great pride long before anything

---

1. 2018

happened there. That's because of a 700-year-old Christmas prophecy. By the time you finish this book, I hope you'll never forget it. Here's the prophecy:

> "But as for you, Bethlehem Ephrathah,
> Too little to be among the clans of Judah,
> From you One will come forth for
> Me to be ruler in Israel."[2]

Here's the next part of the prophecy:

> "And He will arise and shepherd His flock
> In the strength of the Lord . . ."[3]

Notice how Micah says Jesus will be a shepherd. And look at the next part:

> "This One will be our peace."[4]

Everyone in Bethlehem would have known this prophecy.

Their shepherds perhaps felt even more pride than the Bethlehem townfolk because the Messiah was to be a shepherd like them.

But Herod the Great, King of the Jews, didn't know any of this.

When the Wise Men arrived looking for Jesus, Herod assembled the chief priests and scribes.

Here's the passage:

". . . gathering together all the chief priests and scribes of the people, [Herod] inquired of them where the Messiah was to be born."[5]

They told him in Bethlehem and then quoted Micah's prophecy:

> "And you, Bethlehem, land of Judah,

---

2. Micah 5:2, NASB
3. Micah 5:4, NASB
4. Micah 5:5, NASB
5. Matthew 2:4, NASB

JOY

> Are by no means least among the leaders of Judah;
> For from you will come forth a Ruler
> Who will shepherd My people Israel."[6]

Herod didn't know because his heritage wasn't Jewish. His family was from the Edomites, and Edom was hated by the Jews. We'll get to that, and the impact it had on Herod.

But most Jews likely knew that Bethlehem was prophesied as the birthplace of the Messiah, and here's why:

First, Jews were deeply religious, their lives revolved around their synagogue, temple festivals, and worship. Second, because of their devastating history, which we'll examine, they looked forward to the Messiah, their promised Deliverer.

Except, surprisingly, this wasn't true for those in Jerusalem, as we looked at earlier. We'll study more of that story. But for now, know that out of all the Jewish people, those of Bethlehem would have held Micah's 700-year-old prophecy closest to their hearts.

The Christ child would be born in their town, and nothing topped that. Nothing.

Like Florida and Buffalo, those in Bethlehem had something to be proud of. In their eyes, the coming birth of the Messiah made Bethlehem No. 1!

Knowing Bethlehem's pride will become important in the next chapter as you meet the most unlikely of tricksters and those he tried to fool on Christmas Day.

Never heard the Christmas trickster story?

Several years ago, the Lord showed me a treasure hunt that happened on Christmas Day, and I couldn't wait to share it with my readers!

Turn now to the most fun moment in this book and see who outwitted whom the night Jesus was born!

---

6. Matthew 2:6, NASB

Notes, Revelations, Prayers

Date:_____

9. THE SHEPHERDS

THE WORLD'S GREATEST TREASURE HUNT

"And an angel of the Lord suddenly stood near them, and the glory of the Lord shone around them; and they were terribly frightened."

Luke 2:9[1]

---

1. NASB

THE WORLD'S GREATEST TREASURE HUNT

He was a fun-loving angel! Don't take my word for it, let me show you what the Christmas Angel did. This revelation is one of my favorite gifts from God—a discovery about a highly favored angel, chosen by God to announce the birth of our Lord.

Angels Have Personalities

Certain events in history look like angels having fun:

There's the angel who ran a lottery, the one who toyed with Samson's parents, and then there's the impish Christmas Angel. I will cover every angel in the Bible in the upcoming *Angel Editions* of this *Reaching to God* series, and you will see what I mean about God's heavenly beings. They have personalities!

It's well known that the night of Jesus's birth, the Christmas Angel appeared to shepherds. What do we know about these shepherds?

The Christmas Shepherds

Scripture tells us shepherds could be girls, boys, or old men. For instance, young Rachel was a shepherd. Here's the passage:

"While [Jacob] was still talking with them, Rachel came with her father's sheep, for she was a shepherd."[1]

David was also a shepherd. Look at the exchange with King Saul when David wanted to fight the giant Goliath.

"But Saul said to David, 'You are not able to go against this Philistine to fight him; for you are only a youth, while he has been a warrior since his youth.' But David said to Saul, 'Your servant was tending his father's sheep. When a lion or a bear came and took a sheep from the flock, I went out after it and attacked it, and rescued the sheep from its mouth.'"[2]

Moses was also a shepherd, however not as a boy. Look at this passage when Moses was eighty, forty years after fleeing from Egypt.

"Now Moses was tending the flock of Jethro his father-in-law, the priest of Midian, and he led the flock to the far side of the wilderness and came to Horeb, the mountain of God. There the angel of the Lord appeared to him . . ."[3]

So, shepherds were girls, boys, and old men. Really, the possibilities are endless as to who those shepherds might have been. However, I think they were kids. Let me show you why, and then you can decide.

The Game

This is how Scripture says the Christmas Angel appeared to the shepherds, and then what the angel said to them:

". . . there were some shepherds staying out in the fields and keeping watch over their flock at night. And an angel of the Lord suddenly stood near them, and the glory of the Lord shone around them; and they were terribly frightened. And so the angel said to them, 'Do not be afraid; for behold, I bring you good news of great joy which will be for all the people; for today in the city of David there has been born for you a Savior, who is Christ the Lord. And this will be a sign

---

1. Genesis 29:9, NIV
2. 1 Samuel 17:33-35, NASB
3. Exodus 3:1-2, NIV

for you: you will find a baby wrapped in swaddling cloths and lying in a manger.'"[4]

The Christmas Angel is one of my favorite heavenly beings. As the Lord pointed out to me, the angel obviously knew where Jesus was. The angel could have said, "He's at Jimmy Blake's house, corner of East and Main."

Why not?

Some may say the angel was testing the shepherd's faith, to see if they were willing to look for Jesus. I agree. But it also seems like the Christmas Angel was having some fun. Let me show you.

Look again at what he said:

". . . for today in the city of David there has been born for you a Savior, who is Christ the Lord. And this will be a sign for you: you will find a baby wrapped in swaddling cloths and lying in a manger."

The angel was handing out clues, ways to find Jesus. Stay with me. This is great! He gave three:

1. City of David
2. Baby wrapped in swaddling cloths
3. Lying in a manger

Once again, the angel could have simply told them where to find the Child, but where's the fun in that? So the cheerful Christmas Angel decided to have a treasure hunt—the world's greatest treasure hunt. And he chose only this select group of shepherds to play and these clues. Once again:

1. City of David
2. Baby wrapped in swaddling cloths
3. Lying in a manger

That's it. That's all they got.

No star. The Magi got the star. But that was later.

So, the world's greatest treasure hunt began.

The First Clue

---

4. Luke 2:8-12, NASB

"City of David" is the first clue and that's easy. It's Bethlehem, right?

Uh, no.

This came as a surprise to me because the New Testament repeatedly calls Bethlehem the city of David. David lived in Bethlehem as a boy.

But in the Old Testament, which was the only Scripture they had, "city of David" was used to refer to Jerusalem. That's because Jerusalem was where David ruled. And Jerusalem wasn't far from Bethlehem. The shepherds could have walked.

And, frankly, why even say "city of David"? Why not just say "Bethlehem"?

I don't see how you can look at the Christmas Angel in any other way than as a bit of a trickster—hiding Jesus's location from them and also deliberately trying to throw the shepherds off the trail, since "city of David" to Jews was Jerusalem.

Yet out of all the shepherds in the world, these were Bethlehem shepherds. As I said in the last chapter, the people of Bethlehem certainly knew Micah's prophecy some 700 years old, because it was about them!

"But as for you, Bethlehem Ephrathah . . . from you One will come forth for Me to be ruler in Israel."[5]

David belonged to Bethlehem, and the upcoming birth of the Messiah was Bethlehem's claim to fame. I imagine these shepherds must have put their heads together and said, "No. Not the 'city of David' as all of Israel thinks of it. Not Jerusalem."

So, despite the confusing "city of David" clue, the shepherds were certain of one thing—the Christ would be born in Bethlehem.

And that's where they went!

The Second Clue

Arriving in Bethlehem, the shepherds could turn to another clue:

5.

the manger. That narrowed things down. A manger wasn't a baby crib. Merriam-Webster defines it as "a trough . . . in a stable designed to hold feed or fodder for livestock." And not everyone had livestock.

Scholars think there were about 300 to 1,000 people living in Bethlehem at that time. What did the shepherds do when they got there?

You can easily figure this out. The shepherds would have gone from one owner of livestock in Bethlehem to the next.

Once again, the Christmas Angel knew where Jesus was, but isn't this more fun? That's why I think the angel chose young shepherds.

But a manger? This must have been on the minds of those boys or girls. They were looking for a baby, and you know the shepherds were thinking about that manger the whole time.

The long-awaited Messiah, the one destined to lead Israel, in a food trough? Could that possibly be true?

But they find the Child just so.

The Third Clue

The Christmas Angel made sure to give the shepherds a final confirmation. His last clue was a Baby wrapped in swaddling cloths.

In other words, when they found the Baby in the manger, they would know this was, in fact, the Messiah, if the angel's additional words were true—if the Child was also wrapped in swaddling cloths.

And the shepherds then found Jesus just exactly as the angel had described Him. Thus ends the world's greatest treasure hunt.

Delight in the Lord

We are made in the image of a God of joy. My favorite picture of the Lord is called "Jesus Laughing." I wonder how often His words were said with a smile.

We have a truly wonderful God. Why wouldn't He have fun-loving angels? Delight in your faith, treasure being with the Lord, and know that He cares for you.

Also, don't miss His sense of humor.

Notes, Revelations, Prayers

Date:_____

10. THE SWADDLING CLOTHS

A COINCIDENCE OR THE HAND OF GOD?

"You will find a Babe wrapped in swaddling cloths, lying in a manger[1]."

Luke 2:12[2]

---

1. It can also be translated "feed trough."
2. NKJV

AN AMAZING COINCIDENCE OR THE HAND OF GOD?

My friend Catherine told me about the Sunday she hurried upstairs to the church balcony. Normally, she likes to be on the first floor, but she was late that morning.

Once seated, she eyed a newborn in the congregation below her.

"I needed to see something cheerful," she told me. Catherine had just learned that her company was dissolving. She's a single mom and was shaken by suddenly having no job.

Catherine glanced at the baby's parents and realized she knew them. After church, she went to hold the child, and that's when it happened.

"Catherine," the baby's father said. "You're in!"

"What do you mean?" she asked.

"My company is going into your building. I told them about you, and you're in—you don't even have to move your stapler!"

Some would call it a coincidence, but Catherine knew it was the Hand of God.

There are many "coincidences" in Scripture.

Here's one on Christmas Day.

When the Christmas Angel appeared to the Bethlehem shepherds, couldn't he just as easily have chosen the goat herders on a nearby hillside?

No. As you saw in the last chapter, the angel said very little. But did you catch why those shepherds were important to the Christmas story? Look again at his words:

"For there is born to you this day in the city of David a Savior who is Christ the Lord. And this will be the sign to you: You will find a Babe wrapped in swaddling cloths, lying in a manger."[1]

Did you see the reason the angel chose those shepherds?

Let me show you.

Many Christians ignore the Old Testament. They say, "Jesus changed everything." For them, it's out with the old and in with the new.

But the group "Jews for Jesus" has interesting information. Take Rabbi Jason Sobel, who says the Bethlehem shepherds were *Levitical* shepherds.

That looks like a big word, but it's easy to understand.

The third book of the Old Testament is Leviticus. Together with Exodus, it contains the requirements for Jewish sacrifice. For instance, "Your lamb shall be without blemish . . ."[2]

Who do you think was charged with making that happen?

The Bethlehem shepherds—the ones the Christmas Angel came to visit. Rabbi Sobel says in a video posted online on December 23, 2017, that these Levitical shepherds provided the temple with the sacrificial lambs.

On Christmas Day, as those shepherds knelt in awe before baby Jesus, they must have noticed a remarkable coincidence: The Lord was wrapped in swaddling cloths. The same swaddling cloths they used to wrap the newborn lambs to keep them from spot or blemish.

As you can see, God had well-planned Christmas Day.

At the birth of Christ, He quietly announced that Jesus would become the sacrificial Lamb.

---

1. Luke 2:11, 12, NKJV
2. Exodus 12:5, ESV

JOY

But this is where it could get confusing for the Jews.

First-century Jews were deeply religious. They would have known that some 700 years earlier, Isaiah had prophesied two things.

First, "The voice of one crying in the wilderness, 'Prepare the way of the Lord.'" Second, Isaiah Chapter 53, prophesying that Jesus would be "led as a lamb to the slaughter."[3]

I say confusing because how can Jesus be both the Lord who was to deliver Israel and also be a lamb led to slaughter? It would take some 700 years for these two prophecies to make sense.

Roughly thirty years after the shepherds found Jesus, John the Baptist knew that he had been chosen to fulfill the first prophecy. He was "the one crying in the wilderness, 'Prepare the way of the Lord.'"

John had then baptized the Messiah.

But, amazingly, John the Baptist also knew the meaning of the second prophecy—that the Lord would be sacrificed. Look at what he said after baptizing Jesus:

"The next day [John] saw Jesus coming to him, and said, 'Behold, the *Lamb of God* who takes away the sin of the world!' . . . the next day John was standing with two of his disciples, and he looked at Jesus as He walked, and said, 'Behold, the *Lamb of God*!'"[4] I added the emphasis so you would see it clearly. John knew Jesus would be sacrificed.

That moment is a truly breathless and beautiful moment.

But the disciples only understood the first part. That Jesus was the Messiah:

"One of the two who heard John speak, and followed [Jesus], was Andrew . . . He first found his own brother Simon and said to him, 'We have found the Messiah . . .'"[5]

They did not understand Isaiah 53—how the Messiah could also be the sacrificial Lamb. That's because they believed, as did almost every-

---

3. Isaiah 40:3; 53:7 NKJV
4. John 1:29-36, NASB
5. John 1:40-41, NASB

one, that the Deliverer for Israel would free the Jews from their Roman rulers.

But John the Baptist knew what the Deliverer meant. John said, "Behold, the Lamb of God who takes away the sin of the world!"

John knew Jesus must be crucified. But Peter fought Jesus when the Lord tried to explain this to His disciples. Here's the passage:

"From that time Jesus began to point out to His disciples that it was necessary for Him to go to Jerusalem . . . and to be killed, and to be raised up on the third day. And yet Peter took Him aside and began to rebuke Him, saying, 'God forbid it, Lord! This shall never happen to You!'"[6]

We understand that Jesus was the Lamb led to the slaughter, but only because we're Monday morning quarterbacks. We know what the disciples didn't understand as they walked with Jesus. We know the Crucifixion must happen, and we know the Resurrection followed.

But the disciples didn't know any of this.

Once Jesus was crucified and raised from the dead, only then did Isaiah's prophecies make sense. Jesus was both the Deliverer and the lamb led to slaughter!

So even though the Bethlehem shepherds probably didn't understand what they saw that night, God deliberately chose them.

It wasn't a coincidence.

They swaddled the newborn lambs for sacrifice just as the Lord was swaddled at His birth, announcing that He was the Lamb of God without blemish, destined to be sacrificed.

Like those shepherds, you may experience something astonishing and perhaps not understand for decades what God was doing in your life. Or the Lord's handiwork may be as clear as Catherine's new job that bright Sunday morning.

Be on the lookout for what God is telling you. Listen and watch closely.

God speaks through amazing "coincidences."

---

6. Matthew 16:21-22, NASB

Notes, Revelations, Prayers

Date:_____

11. THE OLD MAN OF CHRISTMAS

THE NAUGHTY OR NICE LIST

"If we confess our sins, He is faithful and just to forgive us . . . and to cleanse us from all unrighteousness."

1 John 1:9[1]

"...the blood of Jesus, His son, cleanses us from all sin."

1 John 1:7[2]

---

1. ESV
2. ESV

THE NAUGHTY OR NICE LIST

Every two-year-old knows what's up. Just ask one. They'll warn you. They'll sternly tell you about Christmas—getting on the wrong list is a no-no.

Because the naughty and nice suffer different fates.

It's always been so.

Look at the very first Christmas—the nice received some pretty great gifts. First, consider Zechariah and Elizabeth, an elderly couple. The two were righteous before God and their dream came true—a son.

This was John the Baptist, who would herald the coming of the Messiah.[1]

Next, there was Joseph, a very special man indeed, and Mary, whom God adored. The angel Gabriel told her: "Greetings, you who are highly favored!"

Gabriels said it twice. "Mary, you have found favor with God."[2]

She and Joseph received the greatest Christmas gift of all time—baby Jesus, the Son of God.

The third group was the Bethlehem shepherds.

---

1. Luke 1:5-80
2. Luke 1:28, 30, NIV

The angels told them: "Glory to God in the highest, and on earth peace to those with whom He is pleased."[3]

Pay attention. The angels didn't say, "Peace to all."

No.

They said, "Peace to those with whom He is pleased." The shepherds were on the nice list—very good shepherds. Their gift was seeing the Messiah first.

Who was next? The old, old man of Christmas.

Let's see if you remember him from your many years of reading the Christmas story. Was that:

1. Santa Claus
2. King Herod
3. Simeon
4. Hosea

Take a close look and choose your answer. Who received the best gift after the shepherds?

I'll narrow it for you:

Not Santa Claus. The story of the bearded gent is nowhere in Scripture—Santa probably came from a wealthy 4th-century man named Nicholas, who gave gifts to the poor.

The Bible's very old man in the Christmas story is someone entirely different. No red suit, reindeer, or presents.

If you look at Scripture, the next event after the shepherds is the circumcision of Jesus when he was eight days old. That happened at the temple.

Then the family returned to the temple for their purification, which was 40 days from the birth of Jesus according to the Law of Moses. Here's the passage:

"At the end of eight days, when He was circumcised, He was called Jesus . . . And when the time came for their purification . . . they brought Him up to Jerusalem to present Him to the Lord . . . Now there was a man in Jerusalem, whose name was Simeon."[4]

---

3. Luke 2:14, ESV
4. Luke 2:21-25, ESV

The answer is No. 3, Simeon.

Few have ever heard about this old, old man of Christmas. More importantly, he clearly wasn't naughty. Simeon was very nice. Scripture tells us four things.

First, Simeon was anointed. "The Holy Spirit was on him."[5]

Second, the Spirit had given Simeon a revelation. "And it had been revealed to him by the Holy Spirit that he would not see death before he had seen the Lord's Christ."[6]

Whoa! That's big!

Simeon must have been very, very nice in the eyes of God.

Third—and this is a downright amazing event. It seems that the Holy Spirit went to Simeon and told Simeon to go to the temple courts: "And [Simeon] came in the Spirit into the temple..."[7]

That's because Simeon was promised he would see the Messiah, as I said, and Simeon was there when Mary and Joseph arrived for their purification.[8]

Simeon then took their baby Jesus into his arms and praised God, saying, "Sovereign Lord, as you have promised, you may now dismiss your servant in peace. For my eyes have seen your salvation . . ."[9]

Simeon's interaction with Jesus is such a beautiful moment in Scripture, and an amazing gift to him from God. Unfortunately, this passage is often overlooked.

And there's more. Simeon also had a painful prophecy.

He said to Mary, "This child is destined to cause the falling and rising of many in Israel, and to be a sign that will be spoken against, so that the thoughts of many hearts will be revealed. And a sword will pierce your own soul too."[10]

What Simeon knew that day, Mary would not understand for three more decades. Not until the Crucifixion and Resurrection.

---

5. Luke 2:25, ESV
6. Luke 2:26, ESV
7. Luke 2:27, ESV
8. Luke 2:27, ESV
9. Luke 2:29-30, NIV
10. Luke 2:34, 35, NIV

When you look at these people, you may feel you belong on the naughty list. That your sins are too great.

No. Not true.

David committed adultery with Bathsheba and then ultimately ordered the murder of her husband. It was wholesale evil.

Some would say that David belonged on the naughty list forever! But that's not what happened.

Why? Here it is: Because David loved God more than anything. That's what matters.

David repented, sought to live righteously, and God blessed him.

Listen to me. It's not the falling down that counts—it's that you return to God on your knees.

No matter how many times you fail Him, get up and go to God. Show your heavenly Father that you sincerely want to change.

"If we confess our sins, He is faithful and just to forgive us . . . and cleanse us..."[11] Powerful words. Read them again. "If we confess our sins, He is faithful and just to forgive us . . . and to cleanse us..."

You only need that verse and this one: "The blood of Jesus, His son, cleanses us from all sin."[12]

In the Bible's Christmas story, an angel told Joseph that Jesus came to save us. Here's the passage: "Joseph, son of David, do not fear to take Mary as your wife . . . She will bear a Son, and you shall call his name Jesus, for he will save his people from their sins."[13]

Jesus is your Christmas gift, now and always.

There are no perfect people. We're all in need of a Savior—everyone needs help.

Seek holiness. Go to God. Talk to Him. Confess your wrongs, and praise Him. Learn to meditate and study Scripture.

Any two-year-old can tell you—the nice get the good stuff. Those who love the Lord and seek to please Him receive God's greatest blessings.

---

11. 1 John 1:9, ESV
12. 1 John 1:7, ESV
13. Matthew 1:20-21, ESV

Notes, Revelations, Prayers

Date:_____

12. ANNA

LIKE FATHER, LIKE DAUGHTER

Jesus says, "You did not choose Me, but I chose you."

John 15:16[1]

---

1. NIV

LIKE FATHER, LIKE DAUGHTER

What's in a Name?

When I first moved into my neighborhood, I didn't know Melanie, my across-the-street neighbor, but I passed her house every day.

It seemed like there was always a different animal coming and going. Eventually, I realized that Mel is more or less the Humane Society of the neighborhood. She takes in what no one wants.

The newest arrival is a beautiful black baby rooster.

"Don't the cats care?" I asked, as we sat on my patio on a Sunday afternoon, catching up.

"They all get along," she said with a shrug.

I suddenly remembered how my sick little dog used to like to go over there and be with whatever furry creatures were on her porch. I guess there's an unspoken acceptance among her animals—all were lost and now have a home.

"But doesn't he miss the chickens?" I asked about the baby rooster.

"Well, if he does," she said, a bit indignantly, "he's free to go anytime he wants. We're not stopping him."

It was sort of funny because I knew Mel was treating that baby rooster really well—grapes and celery. Every day was Thanksgiving for the sweet little guy. He wasn't going anywhere.

I told her I wanted to write about him but didn't want to tattle on his whereabouts.

"Do you think whoever owns him will come and get him?" I asked.

She didn't seem concerned. "They'll have to catch him first."

Again, I laughed. I know nothing about roosters.

They named him *Scratch*.

Far be it from me to tell my neighbors what to call their pets, but *Scratch*? For a silky black beauty?

Names in Scripture can also be surprising. Take Jacob, whose name means "heel-grabber," because Jacob had grasped the foot of his twin as they were born.

The interesting part about Jacob is that his name changed.

Although this name change happened nearly 2,000 years before the birth of Christ, that scene finds its way into the Christmas story.

Here's the moment when Jacob shifts in the eyes of God.

A Wrestling Match

You need a little bit of history. Abraham is the oldest of the patriarchs of our faith. God led him to the Promised Land, where he had Isaac, who had Jacob and Esau.

Jacob, born second, tricked his father and stole his brother's birthright. Esau then swore to kill him. So Jacob's parents sent him far away to his mother's family.

Years later, as Jacob returned home with his two wives and children, Jacob learned that his brother was fast approaching with 400 men. Remember, Esau had once wanted him dead.

Terrified for his family, Jacob stayed up all night and ultimately wrestled with God. I am not telling you that Jacob argued with God, but instead, he physically wrestled with the Lord.[1]

Finally, God said to Jacob, "Let me go, for the day is dawning."

---

1. Jacob 32:6-31. I will explain this well-known passage in greater detail in a later book

The ancients believed if you saw the face of God, you would die. But Jacob would not let go. Not until God blessed him.

All that Jacob loved was at stake!

And God did just that, blessing Jacob.

That's how Jacob ended up with a new name—perhaps the most memorable in the Bible. God called him "Israel," which means "one who contends with God."

I told you this moment finds its way into the Christmas story. Let me show you.

Penuel/Peniel

After Jacob wrestled with the Lord, Jacob called the place *Penuel/Peniel*. Here's the Scripture passage:

"So Jacob named the place Peniel, for he said, 'I have seen God face to face, yet my life has been spared.' Now the sun rose upon him just as he crossed over Penuel . . ."[2]

Even though you have both Peniel and Penuel in this passage, they appear to be essentially the same word.[3]

It's because Jacob said, "I saw God face to face, and yet my life was spared," that the words Penuel/Peniel mean "Face of God."

I point this out because the final person Luke mentions in his Christmas story is Anna, a widow.

Luke doesn't tell us about her husband, as you would expect. Instead, Luke tells us about her father. Here it is:

"And there was a prophetess, Anna, the daughter of Phanuel. . ."[4]

Luke wrote in Greek, and Phanuel is the Greek transliteration for the Hebrew word Penuel/Peniel.

---

in this series. There are wild explanations for what happened as Jacob wrestled with God, and they are completely unnecessary.

2. Genesis 32:30-31, NASB

3. This is a bit technical. Peniel is spelled slightly differently from Penuel in the Hebrew. One has the letter Yud and the other the letter Vav. These letters will switch in Hebrew for anyone wondering if it matters that in the passage it reads both Penuel and Peniel.

4. Luke 2:36, NASB. In other versions, like the NIV, it is spelled differently.

So, Anna's father's name meant "Face of God."
That's about to become important.

Anna the Prophetess

Luke closes his Christmas story with Anna. But who was this woman?

Anna seems to have been well-known and well-respected among the Jewish people for three reasons. First, Luke tells us she was a prophetess, so she had a special relationship with God.

Second, she was widowed at a young age. And finally, now in her eighties, Anna devoted herself to God.

Here's the passage:

"And there was a prophetess, Anna, . . . She was advanced in years and had lived with her husband for seven years after her marriage, and then as a widow to the age of eighty-four. She did not leave the temple grounds, serving night and day with fasts and prayers."[5]

So the woman was well known to the people of Jerusalem, where the temple was located. But it's what Anna did with Jesus that garnered Luke's attention.

When the prophetess saw Simeon holding the Baby, she immediately knew who He was. Look at the Scripture passage:

"And [Mary and Joseph] were amazed at the things which were being said [by Simeon] . . . And Simeon blessed them . . . And at that very moment [Anna] came up and began giving thanks to God . . ."[6]

Yet it wasn't just that Anna recognized baby Jesus and praised God. There's more. She's important to Luke because of what she said.

Anna's Prophecy

Luke's passage about Anna continues:

"And at that very moment [Anna] came up and began giving thanks

---

5. Luke 2:36-37, NASB
6. Luke 2:33-38, NASB

JOY

to God and *continued to speak about Him to all those who were looking forward to the redemption of Jerusalem.*"[7]

I added the emphasis so you could see the prophecy, since those words don't look like anything special. However, this is an explosive moment.

I will show you in the Prophetess Chapter just what the prophecy means, and why Luke had good reason to close his Christmas story with Anna.

But for now, look at the beautiful symmetry here.

Unlike the rooster named *Scratch*, Anna's father was given an exquisite name—Phanuel, meaning *Face of God*.

Is it a coincidence that Anna's father would be named Face of God over a century before Anna would see the Face of God?

No. That was a deliberate decision by the Lord.

Anna, born to a man named Face of God, would ultimately see the Face of God before she died.

Listen to me. The Lord chooses whom He chooses. Jesus said, "You did not choose Me, but I chose you."[8]

Some, like this prophetess, receive very special blessings.

Stay close to God and, believe me, you will receive yours.

---

7. Luke 2:38, NASB, emphasis added
8. John 15:16, NIV

Notes, Revelations, Prayers

Date:_____

13. THE MAGI

A STAR, A MANGER, AND GIFTS

"Where is He who has been born King of the Jews? For we saw His star in the east and have come to worship Him."

Matthew 2:2[1]

---

1. NASB

A STAR, A MANGER, AND GIFTS

The Magi Arrive in Jerusalem

The Magi arrive in the Christmas story at a time when Mary and Joseph needed them. It's no coincidence.

But much is misunderstood.

Consider the star that led the Magi. Many imagine three beautifully dressed Wise Men, seated on camels, looking up to the heavens, following that star as they cross the desert from the Far East to Jerusalem.

But that's not what Scripture says.

The Magi could have been two men or a group of fifty. We don't know. Nor does Scripture say they followed the star to Jerusalem. Here's the passage:

"Now after Jesus was born in Bethlehem of Judea in the days of Herod the king, behold, magi from the east arrived in Jerusalem, saying, 'Where is He who has been born King of the Jews? For we saw His star in the east and have come to worship Him.'"[1]

That's not a lot of information. We only know that the Magi eyed

---

1. Matthew 2:1-2, NASB

the star when they were in the East, decided the location was in the region of Judea, and then arrived in Jerusalem. There's no indication that the star led them to Jerusalem, and it definitely didn't lead them to Jesus, because they stopped, apparently lost, and looked for guidance.

Those two verses are a lot to take in at once. Feel free to go back and read what the Bible actually says about the Magi, because Christmas cards, stories, ads, and gifts have definitely formed a solid impression that there were three Wise Men following a star across the desert.

That passage also tells us that Jesus had been born when the Wise Men arrived in Jerusalem: *"Now after Jesus was born . . . Magi from the east came to Jerusalem."*[2]

The Magi then had at least two meetings and left Jerusalem after learning that the king they were seeking was in Bethlehem.

At this point, we're certain the star went before them, guiding the way, but it doesn't look like that beforehand, only that the Wise Men knew the region where the star appeared. Once again, that's because they were lost when they reached Judea and then sought guidance in Jerusalem.

So, now the star guided the Magi from Jerusalem to Bethlehem. And Scripture says they're pretty excited about it: "When they saw the star, they rejoiced exceedingly with great joy."[3]

The star stood in place in Bethlehem, pointing out where Jesus was located. Here's the passage:

"After hearing the king, they went on their way; and behold, the star, which they had seen in the east, went on ahead of them until it came to a stop over the place where the Child was to be found."[4]

As you can see, when the Scripture passage mentions the star again, it doesn't say the star that led the Magi across the desert. It says, "the star which they had seen in the east, went on ahead of them."

---

2. Matthew 2:1, NASB, emphasis added
3. Matthew 2:10, NASB
4. Matthew 2:9, NASB

The Star that Led the Magi

Much has been written about that star, trying to place when it arose and which star it could have been, attempting to tie it to a particular star among the sextillions (not billions or trillions) of the universe.

But do stars we see at night behave in this way? Do they move and shine their light over a certain place?

Look at the picture of the Milky Way[5] on the last pages of this chapter. NASA says it alone is made of 100 billion stars.[6] And the Milky Way is just a speck in the universe.

The Magi followed a star that led them to a specific place. It seems most likely that God didn't pull a star from the universe for that job among the countless observable stars we see at night.

Instead, wouldn't God have created the Christmas Star for this moment in time? A one-of-a-kind star!

The Manger

To finish the passage, Scripture says, "When they saw the star, they rejoiced exceedingly with great joy. And after they came into the house, they saw the Child with His mother Mary; and they fell down and worshiped Him. Then they opened their treasures and presented to Him gifts of gold, frankincense, and myrrh."[7]

Remember that Jesus had already been born when the Magi arrived in Jerusalem. Also, remember that the night Jesus was born, the shepherds didn't keep that to themselves:

"When they had seen Him, they made known the statement which had been told them about this Child. And all who heard it were amazed about the things which were told them by the shepherds."[8]

Moreover, all of Bethlehem knew the prophecy that the Messiah would be born there.

---

5. Creative Commons Canonical URL https://creativecommons.org/licenses/by-sa/4.0/
6. "The Milky Way Galaxy," NASA, December 2015
7. Matthew 2:10-11, NASB
8. Luke 2:18-19, NASB

Clearly, Jesus found a bed that night. Someone made room for the Messiah, and I'll go so far as to say there was a fight for Him.

So, the idea that the Magi arrived at a house to find the Lord in a manger (a feeding trough) didn't happen. Remember, the passage says they found him in a house.

The Christmas depiction of three Magi standing in a barn looking at baby Jesus in a feeding trough isn't what you should remember. Jesus was in a house, probably the largest in Bethlehem. We don't know how many Magi were there.

You should also discard the idea that Jesus was poor. Let's look at that.

The Gifts

The Magi brought Jesus expensive gifts befitting a king they longed to worship. These weren't gawkers. Scripture tells us the Magi came to worship the newborn king. They said, "For we saw His star in the east and have come to worship Him."[9]

Perhaps you will recall the joke of the pro golfer who spent time playing golf with a sheikh. The sheikh wanted to give him a gift, and the golfer said, "Just send me a club."

What the golfer received wasn't a metal golf club but a deed to a golf club. The sheikh bought the golfer what the sheikh thought was the right gift.

The Magi had traveled a long way to *worship a king.* When you see tiny little boxes in manger scenes, rest assured that the Magi did not bring token gifts. They would have brought great wealth appropriate for a king.

The Flight to Egypt

By the time you finish this book, you'll clearly understand that Herod was a vicious, paranoid ruler who had once lost his kingdom to

---

9. Matthew 2:2, NASB

an enemy nation. That's when Rome gave him the title "King of the Jews," and Herod took a Roman army to recapture Jerusalem. We'll look at that in the next chapter.

So, Herod would have found out about Jesus, even without the Magi. The Wise Men aren't in the story just to tell Herod of the birth of the King of the Jews.

Nor do they alert Joseph that Jesus was in danger. That came from an angel. Here's the passage:

"Now when [the Magi] had gone, behold, an angel of the Lord appeared to Joseph in a dream and said, 'Get up! Take the Child and His mother and flee to Egypt...'"[10]

But the Magi are the key to the timing of the Christmas events. Although Luke nowhere mentions the Wise Men, he included one small detail in his Gospel that guides us. We'll look at that soon.

Throughout this text, I've repeatedly said "it's no coincidence." I said it again at the beginning of this chapter.

It's no coincidence that the Magi brought wealth just before the flight to Egypt. Wealth that would take care of Jesus and His family, providing for them during their time alone in a faraway land.

Father God knew before the beginning of time that His precious Son would be in danger from an evil king. And out of seemingly nowhere, somewhere in the East, Father God brought these enchanting figures with great wealth to provide for His Son, who had to flee one dark night to a faraway land.

God provides just as surely for us.

But you have to listen to Him. Joseph marrying a pregnant virgin was an act of faith, as was fleeing in the night to Egypt with nothing more than a terror-filled dream as guidance. But Joseph knew it was God and he listened.

Make your decisions with the Lord. Pray and listen. Those choices determine the course of your life.

---

10. Matthew 2:13, NASB

Notes, Revelations, Prayers

Date:_____

PEACE

"Glory to God in the highest, And on earth peace among people with whom He is pleased."

Luke 2:14[1]

---

1. NASB

THE PEACE OF JESUS
BORN TO A WAR-TORN JUDEA

14. THE WARS

A CITY IN DISTRESS

"When Herod the king heard this, he was troubled, and all Jerusalem with him."

Matthew 2:3[1]

---

1. NASB

A CITY IN DISTRESS

There's a funny woman on the internet who talks about football, even though she knows almost nothing about it. She makes pictures with stick-figure football players and explains what her husband has told her.

But I learn from her, despite the fact that she always adds, "This is mostly accurate and not at all thorough."

Keep that in mind as you read this chapter. I'm not a historian, and I hope this is mostly accurate.

I understand the historical events in the Bible. The problem is that the Old Testament ends roughly 400 years before the New Testament begins. What happened during those years?

Honestly, if the events in those gap years were taught in Seminary, they weren't taught to me. I roughly know about Alexander the Great, and that Julius Caesar was assassinated. I'd heard of the Maccabean revolt. But I had no idea when or how any of those events related to the birth of Jesus. Not until I began writing this book.

You cannot understand the Christmas story without knowing the history of Israel and the events during that 400-year period.

So, I pieced those four centuries together. Every Christian needs to see what caused the people of Jerusalem to be *troubled* at the news of the birth of Jesus.

Here's the passage:

"Now after Jesus was born in Bethlehem of Judea in the days of Herod the king, behold, magi from the east arrived in Jerusalem, saying, 'Where is He who has been born King of the Jews . . .' When Herod the king heard this, he was troubled, and all Jerusalem with him."[1]

If you were taught, as I was, that every first-century Jew longed for the Messiah, you can see from the passage that the birth of Jesus wasn't celebrated by those in Jerusalem.

Why? That's the question.

A Nation Under Enemy Rule

If you have read my column or my other books, you'll know that Israel has a very checkered past. After Moses led the Israelites to the Promised Land and they invaded to seize it and drive out the inhabitants, there was always trouble.

The fifth book of the Bible, Deuteronomy, ends with the death of Moses, and in the next three of four books, Joshua, Judges, and First Samuel, the Israelites fought to secure the Promised Land.[2]

That didn't happen until the book of Second Samuel. It was King David who finally brought peace to Israel, which lasted through the reign of his son, King Solomon.[3]

But civil war tore the nation in half after the death of Solomon.

The North was ultimately taken into captivity in c.722 B.C. by the Assyrians. The South, where Jerusalem was located, suffered the same fate c.586 B.C. at the hands of the Babylonians.

The only reason there was any Jewish state at all was because the

---

1. Matthew 2:1-3, NASB
2. The book of Ruth is between the books of Judges and First Samuel. It doesn't specifically address the difficulty settling the Promised Land, although it falls in that time frame.
3. The Britannica states that Solomon died 922 B.C., but not all sources agree.

PEACE

Babylonians were conquered by King Cyrus, who knew God. He allowed the Jews to return to Judah, which became Judea. Those Jews then rebuilt Jerusalem and the temple.

Nevertheless, Judea wasn't free. It remained under Persian rule.

Persia was then conquered by Alexander the Great in 322 B.C., and the Jews fell under Greek rule. The Jews were conquered again by the Seleucid Empire 223-167 B.C.[4] and ultimately ruled by Antiochus IV Epiphanes. He's important, as you'll see.

A Free Nation

The Maccabean revolt[5] in 167 B.C. started Judea on a path to becoming a Jewish state, free from enemy rule. The Britannica says, "A quarter-century of Maccabean resistance ended with the final wresting of control over Judea from the Seleucids and the creation of an independent Judea in Palestine."

That freedom lasted about eighty years. The Prophetess Anna and Simeon, who both appear in Luke's Christmas story, were born during that time of freedom.

Roman Rule

Anna would have been in her twenties in c.63/64 B.C., when Roman General Pompey, allied with Julius Caesar, conquered Judea.

Jerusalem now fell under enemy occupation again, and Anna and Simeon's world changed violently over the next six decades.

The Romans were politically unstable, to say the least. Julius Caesar and Pompey vied for control, which led to civil war.

Pompey was assassinated in 48 B.C. in Egypt. Julius Caesar was also assassinated in 44 B.C. in Rome.

---

4. The source is the Britannica.com
5. Britannica claims that King Antiochus declared war on Judaism, which led to a successful revolt by a Jewish priest in 167 B.C.

And thus began a new power struggle between three men, including Octavian and Marc Antony[6], who was a friend of Herod's.[7]

The Parthian Conquest

In the midst of the Roman upheaval, Anna, now in her 40s, and Simeon faced yet another enemy: the Parthians. These mighty Arabs conquered Jerusalem in 40 B.C.

Herod and his brother were ruling by that time,[8] and Herod fled to Rome. His brother died in Jerusalem.[9]

King of the Jews

Herod was named "King of the Jews" by the Roman Senate in c. 39/40 B.C.[10] He returned with a Roman army and took Jerusalem from the Parthians.

Herod exacted vengeance on the city. Estimates range that as many as one in four may have been murdered.

Anna would have been near her 50s now, and you can see how dramatically her life changed in the first century B.C.

All first-century B.C. Jews in Judea of a certain age, including Simeon, lived through that tumult. It colored their lives.

---

6. Eventually, Octavian would declare war on Cleopatra and thus Marc Antony, since the two were together. He defeated them, and the two committed suicide.
7. The fact that Herod survived after siding with Marc Antony and Cleopatra against Octavian, who became Caesar Augustus, says something about Herod. He must have been very intelligent, or else Rome needed him.
8. Herod's father, Antipater, was wealthy and influential and sided with Pompey when he conquered Judea. As a result, Julius Caesar made Antipater procurator (governor) of Judea in 47 B.C.
9. I have read that he was murdered by the Parthians and also that he was tortured by the Parthians and committed suicide.
10. "Some scholars have defended a revised chronology where Herod was named king in 39 B.C., took Jerusalem in the fall of 36 B.C., and died in 1 B.C." Source: Associates for Biblical Research, which reprinted with permission Vol. 66 (2021) of the Near East Archaeological Society Bulletin.

PEACE

A Troubled Jerusalem

Knowing these events, you understand what happened in Jerusalem when the Magi arrived—why everyone was troubled. Here's the passage again:

"Now after Jesus was born in Bethlehem of Judea in the days of Herod the king, behold, magi from the east arrived in Jerusalem, saying, 'Where is He who has been born King of the Jews . . .' When Herod the king heard this, he was troubled, and all Jerusalem with him."[11]

No one wanted more bloodshed, but they must have known it was coming.

Herod was King of the Jews. And Herod was vicious. The people of Jerusalem knew he had murdered three of his sons,[12] two of them roughly three years earlier and one that year.[13]

Herod had also murdered a wife he was said to have loved dearly and her mother.

Because Herod had been appointed by the enemy, Rome, the people of Jerusalem were forced to live under his rule.

It was a city in distress.

The prospect that a baby King of the Jews had been born to challenge Herod's throne would have been very upsetting to those who had survived the bloody return of Herod to Jerusalem.

The Secret Meeting

After the arrival of the Magi, Herod met secretly with the Wise Men. Here is the passage:

"Then Herod secretly called for the magi and determined from them the exact time the star appeared. And he sent them to Bethlehem

---

11. Matthew 2:1-3, NASB
12. Antipater, Alexander, and Aristobulus
13. If it was 4 B.C.

and said, 'Go and . . . report to me, so that I too may come and worship Him.'"[14]

The Magi would have had no idea why Herod needed a secret meeting or why he needed to know when the star had risen. Herod explained that he also wanted to worship the new King of the Jews.

That would have fooled no one in Jerusalem. Obviously, that's why Herod met with them in secret.

The Massacre

Did the city know what was going to happen as soon as the Magi arrived with their news—that the newly proclaimed King of the Jews would be eliminated? Did these Jews realize that if Herod couldn't pinpoint the baby, he would kill all the possibilities?

The massacre of the children[15] in Bethlehem soon followed the arrival of the Magi. I doubt that would have been a surprise to those living in Jerusalem, but you can draw your own conclusion.

Did Jerusalem Already Know of Jesus?

Here's the thing. The Magi are only in Matthew's Gospel, so you get the impression that this was when Herod learned about the birth of Jesus.

But that's probably not so.

If you look at Luke's Gospel, the prophetess Anna had witnessed Jesus when he was brought to the temple as a baby. Because of her prophecy, which she told to every Jew looking forward to the redemption of Israel, speaking both night and day in the temple, it's likely that Herod and Jerusalem already knew of the birth of Jesus.

We're going to examine Anna's words in "The Prophetess" chapter. They were explosive!

---

14. Matthew 2:7-8, NASB
15. The killing of the male infants in and around Bethlehem by Herod has been called both the "Massacre of the Innocents" and the "Slaughter of the Innocents."

Notes, Revelations, Prayers

Date:_____

15. JOSEPH

READY FOR GOD TO SHOW YOU THE FUTURE?

"Trust in the Lord with all your heart and lean not on your own understanding, in all your ways acknowledge Him and He will make straight your paths."

Proverbs 3:5-6[1]

---

1. ESV

READY FOR GOD TO SHOW YOU THE FUTURE?

Have you ever felt strangely drawn to act in some way and only afterward understood why—realizing God had shown you the future?

My grandfather owned a neighborhood grocery store several blocks from their family home. On a dark night, my grandmother suddenly grabbed one of his hats, sensing he was in danger. She shoved her hair beneath it, dressed as a man, and hurried to his store. Charging through the front door, she found a robber with my grandfather.

Immediately, the thief bolted and ran.

This grandmother, my mom's mom, was the Rev. Cora Hughes, an ordained Nazarene minister. Renowned for her faithfulness to God, the Lord showed her the future that night.

Many in the Bible were shown the future.

Elijah knew of the coming drought, Daniel knew of the destruction of the temple, and Samuel knew Saul would lose his kingdom. These were men God chose to do great things.

But perhaps the most important was Joseph, Jesus's father. I'll show you why.

Many will say we know little about Joseph, the father of Jesus. He is in the Christmas story both in Luke's Gospel and Matthew's Gospel.

We see Joseph again when Jesus is twelve, and His mother and father are searching for Him in Jerusalem and find Him in the temple.

That's it—and so, preachers and academics alike will tell you that we know little about this Joseph.

I disagree.

What the Bible tells us is profound. It should take your breath away.

Look at Joseph with your soul, not with your mind. What we see is a man who lived his life close to God, acting on the Lord's guidance until God knew that, when the time came, despite unbelievable circumstances, Joseph would listen to Him.

Two of those incredible moments arise.

First—Mary bearing a Child, who wasn't his, and a dream with an angel saying to take her as his wife. The angel said the Child was from the Holy Spirit.

The what?

Scripture doesn't mince words. The Bible says when Joseph awoke, he committed to her.

Prior to that, Scripture says Joseph had been trying to think what to do with her, but as soon as the angel came to him, he gave it no more thought. He didn't say, "Well, it was only a dream." And one that made no sense.

Second—the nightmare that Jesus was about to be murdered by Herod.

By whom?

The Lord had rested in a lone manger surrounded by the gentle sounds of animals and later in a bed before doting Wise Men. But hidden, imminent evil threatened the Lord.

We know this, but how much did the people of Bethlehem suspect? They probably didn't know about Herod's secret meeting with the Magi. Herod didn't want anyone to know.

Newborn babies, infants crawling on their hands and knees, and toddlers taking wobbly first steps would soon be ripped from their mothers' arms and murdered.

Jesus should have been among them.

PEACE

The angel came to Joseph in a dream saying, ". . . flee into Egypt, and stay there until I tell you, for Herod will seek the young Child to destroy Him."[1]

If you'd had a dream like that, would you have acted on it?

All of the Christmas story, as I said earlier, must have felt bizarre to Joseph—the virgin birth, the shepherds arriving in the night, the wise men bringing unbelievable treasure, the bright star hovering outside above the door.

Why leave such a celebration?

"Just a dream!" his family may have said. "Egypt is a long way. You don't know anyone there. Why go?"

Joseph knew exactly why—God had shown him the future.

Listen to me, Joseph only knew what to do because he had walked hand in hand with God for a lifetime. And that tells you a great deal about Joseph's life. He lived so incredibly close to God that the Lord trusted this man above all others.

The Bible doesn't have to tell us. The strength of the relationship between God and Joseph is obvious.

God had to be sure the father of our Lord would not hesitate, would not doubt the angel in the dream—even for a moment. The life of baby Jesus depended on it.

Joseph arose and fled in the night with Mary and the Lord.[2]

Do you see the level of trust between the two?

It didn't happen overnight. Joseph had shown his loyalty to God for a lifetime, and God had decided He could trust Joseph above all others.

That's big!

There were four dreams in all. The final two were to return from Egypt and then settle in a safe area.[3]

You, too, may be guided by a feeling, a vision, a dream, or a series of events too coincidental to be sheer coincidence.

You may even be led by a miracle.

---

1. Matthew 2:13, World English Bible
2. Matthew 2:14
3. Matthew 1:20; 2:13, 2:19-20, 2:22

Draw close to God every day.

Pray to understand His way of speaking to you. As you learn to see Him leading and then act upon His guidance, trust will develop. It's the kind of trust that my grandmother and Joseph shared with God. The kind that led each to act without question.

"Trust in the Lord with all your heart and lean not on your own understanding. In all your ways acknowledge Him and He will make straight your paths."[4]

The more you trust and act upon God's leading, the more you will be shown.

---

4. Proverbs 3:5-6 NIV

Notes, Revelations, Prayers

Date:_____

PATIENCE

"For God so loved the world, that he gave his only begotten Son, that whosoever believeth in Him should not perish, but have everlasting life."

John 3:16[1]

---
1. KJV

FOR A BAJILLION YEARS
GOD WAITED PATIENTLY TO BRING US HIS SON

16. MIND NUMBING OR AWE INSPIRING?

JESUS'S FAMILY PHOTOGRAPH.

"Be diligent to present yourself approved to God as a worker who does not need to be ashamed, accurately handling the word of truth."

2 Timothy 2:15[1]

---

1. NASB

JESUS'S FAMILY PHOTOGRAPH

Some would call it the most boring part of the Bible. Mind-numbing, in fact. But I hope to change your opinion.

I stand in awe of these verses of Scripture, what I call "Jesus's Family Photograph."

Seventeen verses in all. The Lord's genealogy.

Matthew could have left these people out or placed them anywhere, if he had wanted to. In fact, Luke waits until his third chapter to show us the family photograph.[1]

But Matthew didn't see it that way.

Matthew thought the Lord's heritage was *most* important to the Christmas story. That's why Matthew begins his Gospel with Jesus's family photograph.

Since those in the first century A.D. didn't have cameras, Matthew writes down the names of everyone in the picture. Many will quickly recognize these verses:

"Abraham fathered Isaac, Isaac fathered Jacob, and Jacob fathered Judah and his brothers.

"Judah fathered Perez and Zerah by Tamar,

---

1. Luke 3:23–38

"Perez fathered Hezron, and Hezron fathered Ram. Ram fathered Amminadab, Amminadab fathered Nahshon, and Nahshon fathered Salmon.

"Salmon fathered Boaz by Rahab, Boaz fathered Obed by Ruth, and Obed fathered Jesse. Jesse fathered David the king."[2]

That's the first of three groups, roughly 14 to a group. If you know their stories, they make for a pretty interesting section of the photo.

Judah and Tamar are in Volume 1 of *Reaching to God,* along with Boaz and Solomon. Trust me, those are great stories!

My mother had a multi-generation photo. Her Great Uncle Will, who lived to be 101 years old, was in the center. A really tall man, dominating the photo, he was born perhaps before the Civil War.

His brother, my grandfather, is in the photo with my mother and my cousin—three generations. I can't imagine having a photo with 14 generations, even knowing the names of that many generations!

I often wonder if this Great Uncle Will had a Great Uncle Will, also 100 years old. That might have dated him to the Revolutionary War.

I think of how easily his stories could have been passed to my grandfather and then to my mom—generations spanning over two centuries.

Wouldn't you want to know your family's history?

But, even better, what if Great Uncle Will's great uncle, born in the 1700s, had told him he would one day have a niece who would preach the Gospel, who would then have a granddaughter who would do the same? That would be my grandmother and me.

We would stand in awe if that had happened. VERY impressive for Great Uncle Will's great uncle!

Yet that very thing occurs in Scripture. Except it isn't Jesus's relatives 200 years back who talk about Him.

No. It's the Lord's great, great, (many great) grandfathers who knew about Jesus. One spoke of the Lord nearly 2,000 years before Jesus was born.

Think about that—it's mind-boggling!

---

2. Matthew 1:2-6, NASB

PATIENCE

Can you imagine a relative of yours knowing about you 2,000 years ago—in the first century A.D.? It's the same thing.

Here's what happened with the Lord's relative. Jacob essentially said to one of his twelve sons, "It's you."

Listen, he had about an eight percent chance of getting that right. Except Jacob wasn't guessing. He was prophesying what had been given to him by God.

Jacob made clear to his fourth son—"Judah, it's you." You are the chosen one out of my twelve sons. From you will come the Messiah. You are the royal line. Here it is:

Jacob said, "The [royal] scepter shall not depart from Judah . . ."[3]

You would think Jesus would have descended from the oldest of Jacob's sons. But, no. Jacob said, "The [royal] scepter shall not depart from Judah . . ."

See what I mean? It's amazing that Jacob knew this.

Many Christians won't read these seventeen verses that Matthew thought were most important to the birth of Jesus. Or, if they do, it's with a yawn.

But such a prophecy should make us stand in awe of our God.

Fortunately, the stories of Jesus's family members were carefully written and passed from one generation to the next. And, like Jacob, some of the relatives told what would happen in the future.

The next fourteen names in Jesus's family photograph focus on the kings who descended from David. Believe me, most wouldn't have fared well on Santa's "Naughty and Nice" list. I'll notate who's who. Although, just to be clear, the good kings weren't always good and at least one bad king became good in one book of the Bible but not in another.

Here's the passage:

" . . . David (great king, who did some awful things) fathered Solomon (good king at first, then very, very bad) . . . Solomon fathered Rehoboam (bad king), Rehoboam fathered Abijah (bad king), and Abijah fathered Asa (good king with issues). Asa fathered Jehoshaphat

---

3. Genesis 49:10, NASB

(good king who made a massive mistake), Jehoshaphat fathered Joram (bad king), and Joram fathered Uzziah (good king who became bad). Uzziah fathered Jotham (mostly good king), Jotham fathered Ahaz (bad king), and Ahaz fathered Hezekiah (very good king). Hezekiah fathered Manasseh (bad king), Manasseh fathered Amon (bad king), and Amon fathered Josiah (good king, but made a mistake that led to his death). Josiah fathered Jeconiah (bad king) and his brothers (bad kings) at the time of the deportation to Babylon."[4]

Knowing the naughty and nice makes it a lot more interesting.

Here is Matthew's final group of fourteen relatives:

"After the deportation to Babylon: Jeconiah fathered Shealtiel, and Shealtiel fathered Zerubbabel. Zerubbabel fathered Abihud, Abihud fathered Eliakim, and Eliakim fathered Azor. Azor fathered Zadok, Zadok fathered Achim, and Achim fathered Eliud. Eliud fathered Eleazar, Eleazar fathered Matthan, and Matthan fathered Jacob. Jacob fathered Joseph the husband of Mary, by whom Jesus was born, who is called the Messiah."[5]

Then Matthew sums up what he's just done for his reader by explaining the grouping:

"So all the generations from Abraham to David are fourteen generations; from David to the deportation to Babylon, fourteen generations; and from the deportation to Babylon to the Messiah, fourteen generations."[6]

Matthew's audience was deeply committed to God and knew Scripture. They heard a name like Hezekiah and thought of how an angel killed more than 185,000 enemy soldiers as they threatened Hezekiah's reign at the gates of Jerusalem.[7] A story passed down from one generation to the next, just as if my great uncles had done the same.

It's all very impressive!

And yet countless Christians dodge that family photo as fast as possible. "Let's skip this," they say.

---

4. Matthew 1:6-11
5. Matthew 1:12-16, NASB
6. Matthew 1:17, NASB
7. 2 Kings 19:35-37

Why?

Because the photograph is filled with people they don't know. Men and women from the Old Testament.

Listen to me. If you think the New Testament is all that matters, you will never meet Jesus's family. They'll be just a boring collection of names for you.

Instead of running from that photograph, run toward it. Pick out someone every week and get to know his or her story. These are often wonderful and touching moments in Scripture. To prove this, I am including two of the Lord's relatives in the next chapter, Boaz and Ruth, the great-grandparents of King David. I want you to see what you're missing if you dodge the Old Testament.

These are wonderful people!

But understand that Matthew deliberately doesn't tell us every name as he goes down the list. He's more interested in putting the ancestors into groups of fourteen. Why?

Apparently, this was so his listeners could remember them. First-century Christians didn't have a coffee table with a Bible on it.

However, there's another reason—something Matthew carefully hides from his readers. I haven't disclosed it here because I feel a bit conflicted, wondering if I should reveal something Matthew didn't want known. He had a reason. I'm going to do a *Reaching to God* volume on the Kings, and the careful reader will be able to put it together.

Even worse than skipping Matthew's family photo, there are Christian teachers who call Joseph the "stepfather" of Jesus.

They might as well mark out the first seventeen verses of the New Testament. If Joseph wasn't Jesus's father, we cannot tie Abraham and David and the rest to Jesus.

The Lord has no ancestors!

The Bible clearly tells us that the Lord had two fathers—one in heaven and one on earth. Remember when Mary and Joseph found Jesus in the temple when He was twelve? Mary said, "Son, why have you treated us like this? Your father and I have been anxiously searching for you."[8] Mary said *father*, not *stepfather*. That stepfather idea is nowhere in Scripture.

As I said, Matthew thought the Lord's family photo was *most* important to the Christmas story. That's because the birth of Jesus didn't just happen.

Beginning thousands of years ago, God told the prophet Abraham of an everlasting kingdom.[9]

God told Isaiah, "And His name shall be called Wonderful . . . Prince of Peace."[10]

Your Bible may have a recent copyright but know that the pages were written thousands of years ago. Most of it, long before the first Christmas.

And those writers told of what was to come.

Pages filled with prophecy, much older than my great uncles. Verses telling us that Jesus would be our gift from a loving God. A God who longs to hold you close.

Jesus shows us who His Father is.

You are not alone. Lift your heart to God. He is with you.

---

8. Luke 2:48, NIV
9. Genesis 17:19
10. Isaiah 9:6, ESV

Notes, Revelations, Prayers

Date:_____

17. BOAZ & RUTH

HE JUST WANTED TO HELP HER

"Give and it will be given to you."

LUKE 6:38[1]

---

1. NIV

HE JUST WANTED TO HELP HER

[Boaz and Ruth are part of Jesus's Family Photograph, which begins Matthew's telling of the Christmas Story. That genealogy was incredibly important to Matthew. I chose to include this chapter to show you that Matthew's picture of Jesus's family was not boring to his earliest readers. It won't be a big yawn for you either, if you get to know the Lord's family.]

Boaz just wanted to help her. That's all it was—at first.

It was spring in Bethlehem, and the fields of gold were ripe for harvest. His men were already cutting the barley when he spotted her working alongside his women, gathering the leftover crop.

"Whose young woman is this?"[1] he asked his foreman and learned that Ruth was a widow from a neighboring country, now living in Bethlehem for a noble reason.

"She has [worked] from early morning until now," the foreman said, "except for a short rest."[2]

---

1. Ruth 2:5, ESV
2. Ruth 2:7, ESV

Immediately, Boaz left his foreman and went to Ruth—she needed to know there was danger in other fields, men who would assault her.

"Keep close to my young women," he said, ". . . And when you are thirsty . . . drink [water] the young men have drawn."[3]

"Why?" She didn't understand his kindness.[4]

Boaz told her that he had learned how her in-laws left Bethlehem during a famine. The sons married and died. So did the father. The old mother, alone now, wanted to return home, and Ruth had left everything to come with her mother-in-law.

Boaz was impressed.

At mealtime, he invited her to eat with them and quietly told his men to leave extra crop behind in the field for her.

When Ruth went home that evening, laden with grain, she told Naomi, her mother-in-law, the day's events.

"The man is a close relative of ours," Naomi said, probably overjoyed. "One of our redeemers."[5]

A redeemer was a relative who could marry a childless widow, like Ruth, so an heir could be born to inherit the land.

Ruth continued working in his fields throughout the harvest, and then her mother-in-law devised a plan to ensure her daughter-in-law's security.

Ruth did as she was told—getting dressed, going to where Boaz and his men were threshing grain, and hiding until nightfall. Once Boaz fell asleep, she uncovered his feet and lay down. Boaz was then startled in the night and realized a woman was at his feet.

"Who are you?" he asked. It was pitch dark.[6]

"I am Ruth . . . spread your wings . . . for you are a redeemer."[7]

Whoa! She's asking him to marry her!

Honestly, when you read this book, you wonder if Naomi was a tad bit crazy. Why didn't they invite Boaz for dinner? Can you imagine

---

3. Ruth 2:8 ESV
4. Ruth 2:10, ESV
5. Ruth 2:20 ESV
6. Ruth 3:9, ESV
7. Ruth 3:9, ESV

PATIENCE

any woman lying down beside her employer at midnight? Then asking him to marry her?

Even Naomi didn't know how this would end. She had told her daughter-in-law, "He will tell you what to do."[8]

Ruth knew Boaz had felt pity for her, but that didn't mean he would welcome a proposal on a threshing floor in the middle of the night. He could say, "Go home!"

What does Boaz do?

He accepts!

"May you be blessed by the Lord," he says. Then Boaz adds something more interesting. "You have made this last kindness greater than the first . . ."[9]

The first was leaving her family to return with her mother-in-law, but how is this proposal a kindness? A poor, young widow wanting a wealthy landowner?

Here it is, listen to what Boaz says. "You have not gone after young men . . ."[10]

Boaz felt bad about his age.

We all have such insecurities—things we can't change, things we feel another may reject. Some are obvious, like age or size, but others are hidden—a disease, a debt, a conviction, impotence.

Boaz is thrilled.

He doesn't care about his work any longer, quickly leaving the threshing floor to fulfill the complicated requirements to marry Ruth.

"Ruth" is the eighth book of the Bible. Is it just a fanciful tale, or did these people actually live?

The writer plainly tells us the answer. Ruth's child is Obed, whose son is Jesse, whose son is David (as in slingshot David who fights Goliath). And David becomes king of Israel.

Ruth and Boaz were real people. They lived over 3,000 years ago. As I said in the Note at the beginning of this chapter, you saw them in

---

8. Ruth 3:4, ESV
9. Ruth 3:10, ESV
10. Ruth 3:10, ESV

Jesus's Family Photograph, which starts both the New Testament and Matthew's Christmas Story.

Boaz helped Ruth and Naomi, expecting nothing in return, but they ended up helping him more. Although Boaz was a successful man, he was unsure of himself.

Perhaps he had resigned himself to a life without marriage.

Jesus said, "Give and it will be given to you." [11]

No matter who you are, God will send people in need. The person you help today may help you tomorrow.

This is God's way.

---

11. Luke 6:38, ESV

Notes, Revelations, Prayers

Date:_____

18. AGE OLD GIFTS

THE PROPHECIES OF CHRISTMAS

"The people who walk in darkness will see a great light..."

Isaiah 9:2[1]

---

1. NASB

THE PROPHECIES BEFORE CHRISTMAS

Christmas is Coming

My neighbor enjoys Christmas, always finding the perfect present for the right person. Like the one she gave her boss, a man who's never looked in a mirror and not loved what he's seen. Mel ordered him socks with his picture printed all over them.

But such thoughtful gifts require a good deal of time and planning, so Mel starts early.

It was on Saturday morning, September 28, that Mel stood at my back door, phone in hand, calling me.

"Wake up!" she said, since her knocking hadn't roused me.

"I'm a-a-sleep," came my very groggy answer.

"Throw something on and let's roll."

"Where are we going?" I stumbled out the back door, my teeth brushed but my hair not.

"Errands," she said brightly.

I should have known what that meant—Christmas shopping.

"I like to do a little at a time," she said as we stepped inside the store. Mel browsed the aisles for inspiration, that perfect gift waiting to be spotted. I left her to find bleach and M&M's.

Neither for Christmas.

I wrote this column on the following Monday, knowing Mel probably had those presents wrapped. Her kids would see them and know what day was coming.

God did the same thing. He also made sure His children knew Christmas was coming, filling the Old Testament with prophecies of the Messiah.

Each a beautiful gift.

Two Prophecies

Look at what Ezekiel prophesied about Christmas.

"I will cleanse you . . . Moreover, I will give you a new heart and put a new spirit within you . . . so you will be My people, and I will be your God. Moreover, **I will save you from all your uncleanness [sins] . . .**"[1]

Now look at the angel who came to Joseph in a dream, probably after Mary returned to Nazareth from three months of celebrating with Elizabeth in the hills of Judea. The angel said the same thing—Jesus would save His people from their sins:

"Joseph, son of David, do not be afraid to take Mary as your wife; for the Child who has been conceived in her is of the Holy Spirit. She will give birth to a Son; and you shall name Him Jesus, for **He will save His people from their sins.**"[2]

Isn't that amazing? Before Jesus was born, the angel repeated the prophecy Ezekiel had proclaimed some 600 years earlier!

Isaiah's Prophecy

Even before Ezekiel, the prophet Isaiah famously said, "Therefore

---

1. Ezekiel 36:25-29, NASB, emphasis added
2. Matthew 1:20-21, NASB, emphasis added

the Lord Himself will give you a sign: Behold, the virgin will conceive and give birth to a son, and she will name Him Immanuel."[3]

Amazing because of how precise those words are. And that was some 700 years before Christmas!

More Prophecy from Isaiah

Isaiah continued with another very detailed prophecy. "... by the way of the sea, on the other side of the Jordan, Galilee of the Gentiles. The people who walk in darkness will see a great light; Those who live in a dark land, the light will shine on them."[4]

Once Jesus was born and returned from Egypt, Scripture says, "and being warned in a dream [Joseph] withdrew to the district of Galilee."[5]

Joseph was warned by God, and that's when he returned to Galilee. Mary and Joseph didn't just end up there with Jesus.

Micah's Prophecy

Micah's prophecy was just as detailed.

Also roughly 700 years before the birth of Jesus, he prophesied, "But as for you, Bethlehem ... From you One will come forth for Me to be ruler in Israel. His times of coming forth are from long ago, from the days of eternity."[6]

Yes, Micah prophesied that Jesus would be born in Bethlehem, as we have seen, but Micah added a lot more, saying that Jesus lived from the "days of eternity."

He was more than a ruler—Jesus was God.

Moses's Prophecy

---

3. Isaiah 7:14, NASB
4. Isaiah 9:1-2, NASB
5. Matthew 2:22, NASB
6. Micah 5:2, NASB

Roughly 1,500 years before the birth of Jesus, Moses wrote the first verse of the Bible and revealed then that Jesus was from the start of eternity.

In English, it reads, "In the beginning, God created the heavens and the earth." But in Moses' original Hebrew, the first words are "Bereshit bara Elohim."

This is important. Moses used the plural word "Elohim" for God. ("Eloah" or "El" is the singular for God.)

In other words, the first three words of Scripture in Hebrew say, "In the beginning (We) created."

God is We—Father, Son, and Holy Spirit. Thus, Jesus's "times of coming forth are from long ago, from the days of eternity," as Micah prophesied.[7]

More Prophecy from Micah

Moreover, Micah said *times*, not *time*, of coming forth. Thus, Micah prophesied appearances of Jesus throughout the Old Testament.

I look forward to showing those to you in this *Reaching to God* series. I think those moments are very special.

More Prophecy from Isaiah

Isaiah also prophesied about a bad place in Israel. "In earlier times He treated the land of Zebulun and the land of Naphtali with contempt, but later on He will make it glorious, by the way of the sea, on the other side of the Jordan, Galilee of the Gentiles. The people who walk in darkness will see a great light;"[8]

Isn't that beautiful?

This is where Jesus chose to live. Here's the passage:

"[Jesus] withdrew into Galilee; and . . . came and settled in Capernaum, which is by the sea, in the region of Zebulun and Naphtali . . .

---

7. Micah 5:2, NASB
8. Isaiah 9:1-2, NASB

From that time Jesus began to preach and say, 'Repent, for the kingdom of heaven is at hand.'"[9]

The Lord became their Light.

Zechariah's Prophecy

And six months before Christmas, when John the Baptist was born to Elizabeth and Zechariah, Scripture says the old priest, filled with the Holy Spirit, proclaimed this prophecy about his son, the prophet, and Jesus:

"Blessed be the Lord God of Israel, for He has visited and redeemed his people and has raised up a horn of salvation for us in the house of his servant David, as he spoke by the mouth of his holy prophets . . . And you, child, will be called the prophet of the Most High; for you will go before the Lord to prepare his ways, to give knowledge of salvation to his people in the forgiveness of their sins, because of the tender mercy of our God . . ."[10]

The Many Gifts of Prophecy

The Lord knew what He was doing long before Jesus was born, giving these gifts of prophecy to His people, one right after another.

I could go on and on.

Some scholars say there are as many as 300 prophecies of Jesus in the Old Testament. God wanted His children to know Christmas was coming!

Don't let anyone shame you for your Christmas plans—even if it includes pulling a neighbor out of bed on September 28 to join your shopping expedition.

Remind those naysayers that God started preparing for Christmas a bajillion years before Jesus was found in a manger—when Father, Son, and Holy Spirit created the heavens and the earth.

---

9. Matthew 4:12-17, NASB
10. Lk. 1:67-78, ESV

God knew then that He would reveal Himself, His great love and mercy, with the birth of Jesus on Christmas Day.

May God be praised!

Notes, Revelations, Prayers

Date:_____

Notes, Revelations, Prayers

Date:_____

LOOKING DEEPER

I included this section for those who like to look at the intricacies of the Bible.

If that's not for you, jump ahead to the Six Gifts.

19. THE EDOMITES

TAKING A STEP BACK

"And gathering together all the chief priests and scribes of the people, [Herod] inquired of them where the Messiah was to be born."

Matthew 2:4[1]

---

1. NASB

TAKING A STEP BACK

Who or What Was Obadiah?

One Sunday morning, I began the sermon, asking, "Is Obadiah a book of the Bible?"

I stopped as the sanctuary fell silent.

"Or was he a king?" I continued. "Maybe Obadiah was a man who washed Jesus's feet."

I paused.

"Or—perhaps Obadiah has no historical significance."

Everyone listened, waiting.

Who was Obadiah? Inquiring minds suddenly needed to know.

"Raise a hand," I said, "if you think Obadiah is important in the Bible."

I waited.

They thought.

A few hands went up, but seemed unsteady. They came back down.

As you read this, what do you think? Does the name Obadiah ring any bells? Should you know it?

I asked the congregation again, but no one wanted to commit. The name was just too obscure.

Listen, Obadiah is a book of Scripture, and as you can see, it's lost in the pages of your Bible.

But who or what was Obadiah? An important place or was Obadiah a person of merit?

Here it is: Obadiah was a prophet, and his vision is the shortest book of the Old Testament. One chapter long.

The Edomites

Obadiah's prophecy is about the Edomites.

The who?

I know. That also takes a second. Who were the Edomites, and why should anyone care? Let me show you.

In Genesis, God made a pact with Abraham, saying the Promised Land would go to the patriarch's descendants. Yet, not to all of them.

Abraham's son Isaac had twins, and Esau, the oldest, fathered the Edomites, while Jacob, the youngest, became Israel.

The little book of Obadiah is a vision of God's fury toward Esau's heirs. The one and only chapter opens with murder.

Mass murder.

These are God's words. "The arrogance of your heart has deceived you . . . though you make your home high like the eagle . . . from there I will bring you down . . . your warriors will be filled with terror . . . so that everyone will be eliminated from the mountain of Esau by murder."[1]

Everyone eliminated by murder? What could the Edomites have possibly done to anger God that much?

Here it is: "Because of violence to your brother Jacob."[2]

It seems that when war broke out against Jerusalem, the Edomites watched. Worse yet, they also participated, harming the Israelites and plundering Jerusalem.

God said, "On the day that you stood aloof, on the day that

---

1. Obadiah 1:4-9, NASB
2. Obadiah 1:10, NASB

strangers carried off his wealth, and foreigners entered his gate and cast lots for Jerusalem—you too were as one of them." [3]

The Lord admonished the Edomites in detail for what they had done, saying, "Do not enter the gates of My people on the day of their disaster . . . do not lay a hand on their wealth . . . Do not stand at the crossroads to eliminate their survivors; and do not hand over their refugees on the day of their distress. For . . . just as you have done, it will be done to you. Your dealings will return on your own head . . . so that there will be no survivor of the house of Esau . . ."[4]

When did all this actually happen, and when was Obadiah's vision?

No one knows, but Edom is specifically mentioned in the Psalms for rejoicing after King Nebuchadnezzar captured Jerusalem and led the Israelites into captivity in Babylon c. 587 B.C. Here it is:

> "By the rivers of Babylon we sat and wept . . .
> Remember, Lord, what the Edomites did
> on the day Jerusalem fell.
> 'Tear it down,' they cried,
> 'tear it down to its foundations!'"[5]

But celebrating Jerusalem's destruction was only part of Edom's misdeeds. Obadiah's vision makes clear that the Edomites actually participated in the Jerusalem invasion, which suggests an earlier war. I say that because Nebuchadnezzar was a fierce king. Ask yourself, would the Edomites have gone anywhere near the terrible Babylonians, much less have scooped up their plunder?

So, Obadiah may be talking about an earlier invasion of Jerusalem.

This much is certain: Jerusalem brought about its own downfall. Northern Israel[6] had already suffered defeat, and God had told

---

3. Obadiah 1:11, NASB
4. Obadiah 1:13-18, NASB
5. Psalm 137:1-7, NIV
6. I use the term Northern Israel, but in the Bible the civil war after the death of King Solomon cut Israel in half. The north continued to be called Israel and the south was

Southern Israel[7] that it would be punished just as severely if the people did not turn from evil.

Jerusalem listened to King Hezekiah, who was led by the prophet Isaiah, but both were long dead by the 6th century B.C. when Jerusalem thumbed its nose at the Lord.

That's when utter destruction befell the city, and Edom rejoiced.

Do Not Gloat

What was the prophet's message? Here it is:

> "Do not gloat over your brother's . . .
> misfortune. And do not rejoice . . .
> on the day of their distress."[8]

Solomon wrote the same in Proverbs: "Do not rejoice when your enemy falls, and do not let your heart rejoice when he stumbles, otherwise, the LORD will see and be displeased . . ."[9]

Yes, in your lifetime, you will be harmed by the acts of others—those who are cruel or steal or lie. Deeds that deserve the anger of God.

Stand down when you see these people reap what they've sown. You may want to rejoice, but back away quietly, lest you ignite the Lord's fury and it descends on you.

"Do not gloat . . ." God says it twice in that book. "Do not gloat . . ."[10]

A big message from the little book of Obadiah.

It's actually also a Christmas message, but in a different way. Be careful with your children. Help them to treat others with respect, as you would treat Jesus.

---

called Judah. To make it easier to understand, I often just use Northern Israel and Southern Israel, but remember that it's actually Israel and Judah in Scripture.
7. See footnote 6
8. Obadiah 1:12, NASB
9. Proverbs 24:17-18, NASB
10. Obadiah 1:12,13 NASB

LOOKING DEEPER

The Christmas season can be a stumbling block if your child gloats over Christmas gifts in front of anyone. Teach them to be careful, not to hurt the feelings of children in families that will have no Christmas.

Herod's Insecurity

But there's more to the Obadiah message. I specifically included the Edomites because of Herod's family.

Britannica.com says that Herod was a Jew.

Technically true, but that's not the whole story. In fact, it's doubtful a first-century Jewish descendant of Jacob would have agreed. Herod belonged to none of the twelve tribes.

He had no Jewish heritage.

Instead, Herod's family members were Edomites. See how important Edom is suddenly becoming to the Christmas story?

It seems when the country of Edom ceased to exist, the survivors moved into the southern part of Judah and the Negev, a semi-arid area farther south.

Since the Jews hated the Edomites, in order to survive in Israel, the Edomites became Jews. They were proselytized—I don't think they had a choice. One "historian," whom I don't trust, said that in 128 B.C., the Hasmonean Jewish king John Hyrcanus conquered them and compelled them to convert to Judaism.

However it happened, Herod was not considered truly Jewish by many Jews.

But Rome wanted Herod after the Parthians seized Jerusalem because Rome proclaimed Herod "King of the Jews."[11] Yet Herod held that title without any Jewish heritage.

Jews were deeply religious, but not Herod. He had to ask for help understanding an important moment in Scripture. Look at the passage:

---

11. You will recall earlier that Herod had just sided with Marc Antony against Augustus, who became Caesar, so it's very interesting that Herod was given this title. Either Herod was incredibly gifted politically, or Rome needed him badly. Maybe both.

> And gathering together all the
> chief priests and scribes of the people,
> he inquired of them where the Messiah
> was to be born. They said to him,
> 'In Bethlehem of Judea . . .'[12]

Herod now knew that this Bethlehem birth was the fulfillment of prophecy, giving it great legitimacy with the Jews.

Also, remember that the Magi called this baby the "King of the Jews." Here's the passage:

> Now after Jesus was born in Bethlehem
> of Judea in the days of Herod the king,
> behold, magi from the east arrived in
> Jerusalem, saying, 'Where is He who has
> been born King of the Jews'?[13]

That was Herod's title.

Herod didn't understand the Jews he ruled—he didn't know their heritage and didn't know their Scripture.

But Herod did know they could turn violent, willing to give their lives for their faith. He knew the Jews could seize his kingdom because it had happened in the Maccabean revolt.[14]

Herod's Edomite heritage is important because it would have been a source of his insecurity with the Jews he ruled. In part, it explains why he ruled with an iron fist, why he was determined to kill the baby born King of the Jews.

---

12. Matthew 2:4-5, NASB
13. Matthew 2:1-2, NASB
14. King Antiochus IV Epiphanes underestimated the passion of the Jews for their faith. Despite Antiochus' overwhelming military power, which we'll look at, the Jews successfully led the Maccabean revolt beginning in 167 B.C. After a quarter century of resistance, the Jews gained control of their nation for roughly 80 years.

Notes, Revelations, Prayers

Date:_____

20. THEOPHILUS

WHY DOES LUKE OMIT THE MAGI?

"Since many have undertaken to set in order a narrative . . . it seemed good to me also . . . to write to you in order, most excellent Theophilus, that you might know the certainty concerning the things in which you were instructed."
Luke 1:1-4[1]

---

1. WEB

WHY DOES LUKE OMIT THE MAGI?

His name was Theophilus. Luke calls him the *most excellent* Theophilus. And it is only because of this Theophilus that we have over one quarter of the New Testament—Luke wrote his Gospel and "The Acts of the Apostles" to influence Theophilus.

There's little doubt in my mind that Theophilus was a *very* important Roman. Someone closely tied to Caesar.

Centurions were ranking Romans, and Luke knew one named Julius very well, as you will see. In fact, there's reason to believe Julius wasn't just a ranking Roman, but a *high-ranking* Roman when you see the fine way Paul was treated in Rome for two years. Presumably, due to Julius's intercession.

But Luke set his sights on someone even higher. Theophilus.

This chapter explains why Luke would have left out details from the Christmas story. Specifically, the arrival of the Magi, the massacre of the male infants in and around Bethlehem, and Joseph's flight to Egypt with Mary and baby Jesus. It also explains why Luke closed the Christmas story with Anna the prophetess, who is otherwise an obscure figure. But she wasn't to Luke. She was important, as you will see.

Frankly, Luke wasn't just a historian, but an excellent historian.

Accordingly, it's difficult to believe Luke didn't know of the Slaughter of the Innocents, as the Bethlehem massacre came to be called.

So, why would Luke omit important events from all that he told Theophilus?

The omission, in and of itself, adds to the argument that Theophilus was a prominent Roman. I'll explain this.

First, let's look at Julius.

Julius

Julius is a little-known figure in Scripture. He was the centurion who took Paul to Rome, some sixty years after the birth of Jesus. We know the time because of Felix.[1]

Luke was apparently Paul's attending physician because he was allowed to travel with Paul. But there might have been other reasons for Luke being allowed on this trip.

Since the voyage happened some sixty years after the birth of Jesus, why is it in a Christmas book? Because it may tell us why Luke failed to record important Christmas events.

Ones he would have known.

Julius, the centurion, was charged with escorting multiple prisoners to Rome, including the Apostle Paul, on a voyage of more than 2,000 miles.

Understand that Paul wasn't in trouble with the Romans.[2]

No, it was the Jews who wanted him dead, so badly that they had earlier tried to ambush and kill him.[3]

In the midst of that turmoil, Paul became a Roman prisoner. I'll let you read those passages in Acts for further clarification, but it was Paul who sought a hearing with Caesar.[4]

A Trip that Changed Everything

---

1. Felix was governor until c. 58-60 A.D.
2. Acts 21:27-34
3. Acts 23:12-22
4. Acts 25:8-12

LOOKING DEEPER

This long voyage would have been like spending months with Billy Graham. What do you think would have happened?

Indeed, it appears Julius was saved. Why?

This centurion turned Paul loose at one port and let Paul go off on his own to see friends.[5] Losing a prisoner meant death for Julius, but the centurion clearly had come to trust Paul with his life.

That's a big moment in Scripture, not to be overlooked.

By October, they had reached a harbor in Crete, and Paul warned against going farther. Yet, since the harbor was unsuitable for a ship during winter and the owner wanted to sail on, Julius disregarded Paul's words.

Sure enough, the ship got caught in hurricane-force winds. The crew ran ropes around the ship to hold it together and threw cargo overboard, but the storm raged for weeks!

For weeks, not days!

Eventually, the terrified crew decided to escape by lifeboat.

Paul quickly warned Julius not to let that happen, or they would all die. But that meant Julius would have to cut the lifeboat loose from the ship. Such an act in a storm was a very serious crime with a likely death penalty. It's a "Devil or the deep blue sea" moment for the centurion.

What did Julius do?

This time, the centurion trusted Paul's words from God, and Julius cut the lifeboat free.

At daylight, the ship was destroyed, but everyone on board reached the safety of an island where they wintered for three months.

Paul became something of a celebrity with the natives, healing their sick. In return, the islanders ultimately provided Julius with everything he needed to go on to Rome with his prisoners.[6]

When you're caught between two bad choices, seek God's direction and then follow it. Julius didn't listen in Crete, but in that violent storm, Julius followed God's guidance.

---

5. Acts 27:3
6. Acts 27-Acts 28

Learn from the centurion. Never shrug off a warning from God.

What Happened to Paul?

If you remember the centurion in Capernaum whose slave Jesus healed, that Roman military leader had built the town's synagogue.[7]

From that story, we know that a centurion could be a very wealthy and powerful man.

Still, centurions were not all equal in pay and authority.

The only real gauge we have of Julius's high stature in Rome is Paul's outcome.

When Paul arrived in Rome, he did not end up in a dark, damp dungeon filled with vermin. The apostle had a very nice life as a prisoner throughout the ending of Acts. As I said, presumably, that was because of Julius.

Paul had saved the lives of those Roman soldiers when the ship broke apart. Paul had also won favor on an island of natives. And it was that favor that helped Julius get back to Rome with his prisoners intact.

Accordingly, it's little wonder that Julius was grateful. He apparently made arrangements for Paul that were amazing.

The apostle was allowed to rent his own house while he awaited trial. Paul was under guard, but his followers could freely come and visit with him. And Paul preached Christ without any interference.[8]

Pay attention to this: These are Luke's last words in the Acts of the Apostles. "For two whole years Paul stayed there in his own rented house and welcomed all who came to see him. He proclaimed the kingdom of God and taught about the Lord Jesus Christ—with all boldness and without hindrance!"[9]

Look at how Luke says, "two *whole* years," emphasizing the amazing way Paul was treated after the trip.

---

7. Luke 7:1-6
8. Acts 28:16-30
9. Acts 28:30-31, NIV

LOOKING DEEPER

Also, see that the Acts of the Apostles ends abruptly. Almost mid thought. There's no conclusion.

Perhaps that's because Luke didn't need to write more. Maybe his mission with regard to these letters was to save Paul, and that had been accomplished.

Why Did Luke Write His Gospel and Acts?

As I said, Luke tells us very specifically what caused him to pen what ultimately became a large part of the New Testament:

"Since many have undertaken to set in order a narrative . . . it seemed good to me also . . . to write to you in order, most excellent Theophilus . . ."[10]

Theophilus is again addressed at the beginning of Acts:

"The first account I composed, Theophilus, about all that Jesus began . . ."[11]

And Luke's Gospel is fascinating. Scholars refer to it as the most eloquently written account of Jesus's life.

But Luke's writings are very different from Matthew's. It's not just that Luke was a well-educated physician who ultimately traveled with the Apostle Paul. No, Matthew and Luke's reasons for their accounts were completely different.

That's important to know.

Matthew wrote to influence Jews to love Jesus.

Yet that's not true for Luke. The historian didn't pen his two books, "The Gospel of Luke" and "The Acts of the Apostles," to bring people to Jesus. The *only* reason Luke wrote was to persuade one man, *most excellent* Theophilus.

The Most Obvious Reason Luke Omits Problems

---

10. Luke 1:1-4, WEB
11. Acts 1:1-8, NASB

Luke wrote to most excellent Theophilus to win him over, and Luke keeps the Christmas story light and joyful. Pay attention to this.

Unlike Matthew, in Chapter 1 of Luke's Gospel, Luke moves from two angel appearances to the celebration of two women and an old priest.

In Chapter 2 of his Gospel, Luke opens with those reigning at the time and then moves to angels, the treasure hunt, and the presentment at the temple with Simeon and Anna.

I'm telling you, it's all sweet and breezy.

In Luke's account, Joseph and Mary are legally married, although not living together, when she gives birth. There's no mention of her being an unwed prospective mother, as Matthew writes.

There's also nothing in Luke about Joseph ever doubting her.

In Matthew's account, the whole city of Jerusalem is upset at learning of the birth of a new King of the Jews. None of that's in Luke's Gospel—no trouble at all from Herod the Great. He's hardly mentioned!

Mary and Joseph go to the presentment and then go back to Nazareth.

But if you look at my combined timeline of Christmas events earlier in this book, you will see that after this presentment in Luke, when Jesus was 40 days old, it's most likely that this is when the Magi arrived in Jerusalem. Then they went to see Jesus, and left by another way. Then Joseph fled with his family, and the murders of the innocents occurred.

I am not saying Luke was wrong. Not at all.

I am saying he had reason to *leave out* Herod the Great's behavior. Essentially, that's all that Luke was doing—avoiding any disparagement of Herod.

Why?

Remember our earlier history lesson?

Rome had titled Herod "King of the Jews" for a reason—he was trusted with regaining Judea and Jerusalem from the Parthians, and Herod accomplished that feat.

Rome would have remembered him very positively, unlike his son.

Luke could write freely about Herod the Great's son, Herod the tetrarch, because Rome ultimately removed and banished him from the kingdom.

Clearly, Luke was trying to win over Theophilus. There's no doubt about that.

There's also little doubt that Theophilus was a prominent Roman.

Recounting Herod the Great's massacre would have been a slap in Rome's face, and Luke has no desire to alienate Theophilus.

So, the Magi are left out because they lead to the massacre.

Luke then has no reason to tell us of the flight to Egypt. Luke knew, like he knew of the massacre, but Luke had a goal. If that was to move a powerful Roman to help Paul, Luke had a very good reason to simply send Mary and Joseph to Nazareth after the presentment and leave out the arrival of the Magi and all the trouble that followed.

The Only Big Question

The only big question in the timeline is this: When did Mary and Joseph return to Nazareth? If the Magi came following the presentment of Jesus at the temple, it works nicely:

Jesus is born in Bethlehem, He is taken to the temple twice in accordance with the Law of Moses, and then the Magi arrive in Jerusalem. The star leads them to Bethlehem, where Jesus is in a house. The Magi worship Him with gifts and then are warned and leave another way.

The nightmare happens with the angel guiding Joseph to flee. Mary and Joseph hurry across the border with baby Jesus. The Bethlehem male children in and around the city are murdered. Mary and Joseph return to Judea after Herod the Great dies. God then warns Joseph to take his family to settle in Nazareth.

You will have to decide for yourself, but I think the story of the Magi, the Massacre of the Innocents, and the flight to Egypt happened. In fact, there's prophecy that Jesus would be called out of Egypt.[12]

---

12. Hosea 11:1

Accordingly, these three events have to go somewhere.

As I have said, Luke was an excellent historian. So, he would have known about the Magi, the massacre, and the flight to Egypt. Since he couldn't disparage Herod, Luke gives us the best clue as to when the Magi arrived in the Christmas story.

Mary and Joseph were poor, and they gave the offering of the poor for Jesus, the doves. Here's the passage:

"And when the days for their purification[13] according to the Law of Moses were completed, they brought Him up to Jerusalem to present Him to the Lord (as it is written in the Law of the Lord: 'Every firstborn male that opens the womb shall be called holy to the Lord'), and to offer a sacrifice according to what has been stated in the Law of the Lord: 'A pair of turtledoves or two young doves.'"[14]

On the other hand, if the Magi had already arrived with their gifts, the parents could have offered a lamb. This one fact should lead us to believe the Magi arrived after the presentment, and that's when all the trouble started.

As I said, the idea that Luke wrote to Theophilus to help Paul is placed in this book because it explains why Luke omits the problems in the Christmas story.

---

13. A woman was unclean and could not worship for 40 days after giving birth to a son.
14. Luke 2:22-24, NASB

Notes, Revelations, Prayers

Date:_____

21. THE PROPHETESS

WAS IT A TRIBUTE?

"[Anna] continued to speak about Him to all those who were looking forward to the redemption of Jerusalem."

Luke 2:38[1]

---

1. NASB

WAS IT A TRIBUTE?

I placed this chapter, like the former two, in this "Looking Deeper" section for those who want a more detailed study of parts of the Christmas story. This chapter explores why the tribe of Asher is mentioned by Luke and also what Anna's explosive prophecy meant.

If it's not for you, please move on to the next chapter. This section isn't meant for everyone.

The Tribe of Asher

While Luke does not tell us Anna's husband's name, he does tell us that she came from one of the twelve tribes of Israel.

"And there was a prophetess, Anna . . . of the tribe of Asher."[1]

Here's what's known about Asher, and it's surprising.

Asher Was Favored by Jacob and Moses

Jacob had twelve sons who became the twelve tribes of Israel.

---

1. Luke 2:36, NASB

Remember, Jacob's name was changed to Israel. His eighth son was Asher.

Israel did not speak well of all of his children, and they received different blessings from their father. The first three, Reuben, Simeon, and Levi, heard the old man's wrath as Jacob was about to die.

"Reuben, you are my firstborn . . . you shall not have preeminence, because you went up to your father's bed; then you defiled it . . ."[2]

It seems that Reuben had relations with one of Jacob's slave-wives.[3]

Jacob then said, "Simeon and Levi are brothers; their swords are weapons of violence. Let me not enter their council . . . for they have killed men in their anger. . . Cursed be their anger, so fierce . . . for it is cruel. I will scatter them."[4]

Simeon and Levi had nearly caused the slaughter of their family when the two murdered all the men of a city to avenge their sister.[5]

But Asher received a favorable blessing from Israel. "As for Asher, his food shall be rich, and he will yield royal delicacies."[6]

Moreover, centuries later, Moses also favored Asher, saying, "Most blessed of sons be Asher; let him be the *favorite* of his brothers, and let him dip his foot in oil."[7]

I added emphasis to one word in the verse so you wouldn't rush past it. Let Asher be the *favorite* of the twelve tribes of Israel.

Now that's a little-known verse.

Who has even heard of the tribe of Asher? Much less considered it as the favorite of the twelve.

When the Promised Land was divided before the invasion, Asher's descendants received the region that sat along the northern coast of Israel. However, that tribe was lost when Assyria conquered Northern

---

2. Genesis 49:3-4, NASB
3. Genesis 35:22
4. Genesis 49:5-7, NIV
5. Genesis 34:25-27
6. Genesis 49:20, NASB
7. Deuteronomy 33:24, ESV, emphasis added

Israel in c.722 B.C. The Assyrians took many Jews into slavery and then repopulated Northern Israel and the land given to Asher.

If the land of Asher no longer existed, why does Luke mention Asher in this passage about Anna's father?

The tribe of Asher gives Anna something Herod didn't have and couldn't buy. The prophetess had a bona fide Jewish heritage, since she descended from one of the twelve tribes.

But perhaps there's more to it since we now know that Asher was favored by both Jacob and Moses. Maybe belonging to the tribe of Asher gave Anna's family prestige among the Jews.

In other words, it's like telling someone your address, and they judge you by whether you live in a bad, good, or great neighborhood.

Anna's family had come from the best neighborhood.

The Prophecy

Remember that Anna is the last person mentioned by Luke in his Gospel. He carefully tells us what she did after seeing Jesus. As we discussed earlier, Simeon had just prophesied about Jesus as he held the Baby in his arms in the temple. Scripture then says:

"And there was a prophetess, Anna . . . She was advanced in years . . . a widow . . . She did not leave the temple grounds, serving night and day with fasts and prayers. And at that very moment she came up [to Jesus] and began giving thanks to God, and continued to speak about Him to all those who were looking forward to the redemption of Jerusalem."[8]

As promised, you will see how explosive Anna's prophecy was at that time. Scripture says, ". . . [Anna] continued to speak about Him to all those who were looking forward to the redemption of Jerusalem."

You can rush over those words. But stop. What does she mean when she says, "looking forward to the redemption of Jerusalem"?

Let me show you.

Earlier, we saw that Jesus was born into a political climate far

---

8. Luke 2:36-38, NASB

worse than what we've seen in this nation—Herod had lost power and, upon his return, murdered countless people.

He was bent on revenge.

And the people of Jerusalem were afraid of him.

Yet there was one person who was not scared.

Anna was thrilled at the sight of Jesus, and she wanted to tell all who were looking forward to Israel's redemption. Again, what does that mean, "looking forward to the redemption of Jerusalem"?

Freedom.

Anna was speaking of the freedom she'd known as a child and into her twenties. Even those around her, who had not lived during that era, all had grandparents or parents who remembered and no doubt talked about a time when there were no enemy soldiers walking the streets of Jerusalem.

Israel's redemption meant kicking the Romans out. It meant freedom from enemy rule.

Could She Have Stated It Differently?

Scripture tells us that when Jesus came to Nazareth, He proclaimed that He was the Anointed One of God. Here's how that happened:

"And He came to Nazareth, where He had been brought up. And as was His custom, He went to the synagogue on the Sabbath day, and He stood up to read. And the scroll of the prophet Isaiah was given to Him. He unrolled the scroll and found the place where it was written,

> **The Spirit of the Lord is upon me,**
> **because He has anointed me**
> **to proclaim good news to the poor.**
> **He has sent me to proclaim liberty to the captives**
> **and recovering of sight to the blind,**
> **to set at liberty those who are oppressed,**
> **to proclaim the year of the Lord's favor.**

And He rolled up the scroll and gave it back to the attendant and sat down. And the eyes of all in the synagogue were fixed on Him. And He began to say to them, 'Today this Scripture has been fulfilled in your hearing.'"[9]

Jesus read the prophecy that Isaiah spoke many centuries earlier.[10]

Anna knew that prophecy. She could have spoken those same words when she saw Jesus—that **the Spirit of the Lord was on Him, the Anointed One who would proclaim good news to the poor, liberty to the captives, recovery of sight to the blind, to set at liberty those who were oppressed, to proclaim the year of the Lord's favor.**

It was a safer way to state her prophecy in the face of Herod's dangerous rule. But that's not what she said.

She did not repeat Isaiah's prophecy as Jesus did some 30 years later. Anna said the Baby would bring freedom. And not just any freedom. Anna said He was the redemption of *Jerusalem*!

Look at it again. She was in the temple in Jerusalem speaking to Jews who either lived in the city or had come there to worship God.

"[Anna] came up and began giving thanks to God and continued to speak about Him to all those who were looking forward to the redemption of Jerusalem."[11]

Anna's Target

Anna knew what she was getting into.
She knew who reigned from the city of Jerusalem. Herod.
The "redemption of Jerusalem" meant deposing Herod.
She made her prophecy a personal threat to Herod!

---

9. Luke 4:16-21, ESV
10. Isaiah 61:1-2, ESV:
    "The Spirit of the Lord God is upon me, because the Lord has anointed me to bring good news to the poor; He has sent me to bind up the brokenhearted, to proclaim liberty to the captives, and the opening of the prison to those who are bound; to proclaim the year of the Lord's favor . . ."
11. Luke 2:38, NASB

Moreover, proclaiming the ousting of Herod and the Romans was treason!

Over and Over Again

Anna didn't do it once. Remember what Scripture says:
"And there was a prophetess, Anna . . . She did not depart from the temple, worshiping with fasting and prayer night and day."[12]

Once she saw Jesus, she spoke her prophecy continuously. Over and over again. Look at the passage:

"[Anna] . . . continued to speak about Him to all those who were looking forward to the redemption of Jerusalem."[13]

This prophetess, from the tribe of Asher, was in the temple night and day, and she spoke about Jesus to everyone she saw who hoped for freedom from the Romans.

Did that put Anna in danger?

Jesus was only a newborn, and yet Herod slaughtered any male infant who could possibly be the King of the Jews. He destroyed babies. No one was going to threaten his throne. Not even an infant.

And Anna did just that when she proclaimed the "redemption of Jerusalem."

She was a brave woman, and it's doubtful she survived Herod's wrath. I don't see how you can look at that passage any other way.

Luke could not say what a demon Herod the Great was in his writings to Theophilus, as we just saw. But Luke could write of the woman who stood up to Herod and most likely died at his hand.

Is this the reason Luke closed his Christmas story with Anna?

Was it a tribute?

Our Political Climate

I originally wrote these words at a time when the political environ-

---

12. Luke 2:36-37, ESV
13. Luke 2:38, NASB

ment in this nation was hostile to God. Years when there was no longer religious free speech in America.

I lived through those years, and so did you. A person could be destroyed for saying or writing God's truth.

Even fearful Christians in my church wanted me to quiet down. It was a painful, alone time for those who held Scripture dear.

Will the church be persecuted again in this country? Undoubtedly.

When the Lord moves you to stand with Him, remember this 84-year-old woman's courage. If you're certain it's God who is leading you, follow His guidance.

Notes, Revelations, Prayers

Date:_____

22. EGYPT

THE SOJOURN IN EGYPT

"But when Herod died, behold, an angel of the Lord appeared in a dream to Joseph in Egypt..."

Matthew 2:19[1]

---

1. NASB

THE SOJOURN IN EGYPT

How long was Jesus in Egypt? No one knows for sure, but the return to Israel was prompted by the death of Herod. Scripture tells us that an angel appeared in a dream to Joseph while he was in Egypt and told him to return. Here's the passage:

"But when Herod died, behold, an angel of the Lord appeared in a dream to Joseph in Egypt, and said, 'Get up, take the Child and His mother, and go to the land of Israel; for those who sought the Child's life are dead.' So Joseph got up, took the Child and His mother, and came into the land of Israel." [1]

Although we don't know the year this happened, since the catalyst for the return to Israel was the death of Herod, the question is, when did Herod die?

The initial problem is that ancient sources aren't reliable. Josephus, for instance, is not a trustworthy historian.[2]

Herod's death is dated anywhere from 6 B.C. to 1 B.C.

But a simpler way to know how long Jesus was in Egypt is to look

---

1. Matthew 2:19-21, NASB
2. If you are reading these chapters out of order, see the earlier chapter on Josephus for an explanation.

at how Herod died. Research concludes that Herod the Great most likely had kidney failure.

Poisoning can bring on kidney failure. If Herod was poisoned, he may have died soon after the massacre of the infants in Bethlehem.

Here's my theory.

Herod was a butcher and deeply hated. After the Parthian invasion, Herod murdered those he thought had not been loyal to him. He wanted the Jews to fear him and they did. So much so that when the Magi announced the birth of the King of the Jews, the long-awaited Messiah, the city of Jerusalem could not rejoice. The people were troubled.[3]

They were afraid.

But it's an entirely different matter to murder an infant.

Herod did that. Not to one child or two, but to all the male babies in the city of Bethlehem and the surrounding region.

I ask you, did it spark outrage?

In "A City in Distress," we briefly looked at another moment of unbelievable affront. King Antiochus had declared war on Judaism, specifically forbidding the worship of God "on pain of death."[4] And that led to a successful revolt by a Jewish priest in 167 B.C.

This was an impossible undertaking.

The Jews hadn't known freedom from enemy rule since the days of King David and King Solomon. That was over seven hundred years.

But there are moments in time that spark outrage. Here's one of those moments with King Antiochus:

"In the Temple, an altar to Zeus Olympios was erected, and sacrifices were to be made at the feet of an idol in the image of the King."[5]

And the Jewish response:

"Against that desecration Judas Maccabeus . . . led . . . a guerrilla war and several times defeated the generals . . . commissioned to deal with the uprising . . . The fighting spirit of the Jews was all the more

---

3. Matthew 2:1-3, NASB
4. Britannica, Antiochus IV Epiphanes
5. Britannica, Antiochus IV Epiphanes

LOOKING DEEPER

impressive because . . . Antiochus had just demonstrated his might to the world . . . with a grand review of his army: 46,000 foot soldiers . . . "⁶

King Antiochus's acts to destroy the Jewish faith caused the Jews to fight with all they had, willing to lay down their lives against impossible odds for what they held dear.

I ask you again. Did the murders of those babies spark outrage?

It doesn't require a lot of thought to believe there were people in Bethlehem, mothers and fathers, grandparents, uncles and aunts, countless relatives of those slain children, who were willing to lay down their lives to see Herod dead.

Did they poison him?

There have been countless royal poisonings in history. It's generally believed that Artaxerxes III was poisoned in 338 B.C., that Mithridates V was poisoned near 120 B.C., that Roman Emperor Claudius was poisoned in 54 A.D., and the list goes on.

If you believe that Herod the Great's kidney failure came from a revenge poisoning for the massacre of those infants, Joseph may have returned from Egypt with his family within the year after he left.

---

6. Britannica, Antiochus IV Epiphanes

Notes, Revelations, Prayers

Date:_____

SIX GIFTS

"Finally, be strong in the Lord and in the strength of His might."

Ephesians 6:10[1]

---

1. ESV

WHAT WAS GIVEN TO ME, I GIVE TO YOU

I write a newspaper faith column for the Lord each week, which began in 2015.

For this *Christmas Edition*, I went through ten years of writings and hundreds of columns to find the best of what the Lord has shared with me.

As I said at the outset, these are not Christmas stories. They are the Lord's gifts, and each one changed my life.

I give them to you now for Christmas.
Experience the power!

1. AN UNEXPECTED GIFT

WHICH WOULD YOU CHOOSE?

"... as the Lord has forgiven you, so you also must forgive."

Colossians 3:13[1]

---

1. ESV

WHICH WOULD YOU CHOOSE?

One day, without warning, he disappeared. This was the old man who stood on the street corner with his cardboard homeless sign. I mentioned him at the outset in "The Greatest Gift."

As the years passed, I had fed him often. He's always on that same street corner near his residence—he had gingerly confided in me that he lives under the bridge.

Since I drive that way to work, I pass him regularly. When traffic is slow, we have a few extra minutes to catch up.

Now he was suddenly gone, and I was concerned. More worried as day after day passed with no sign of him.

Months later, I was in my vehicle in the middle of three lanes of bumper-to-bumper traffic on the bridge, all stopped at the light.

Suddenly, I eyed a man who looked like my panhandler.

Sort of.

But this man stood on a different corner. Moreover, he was clean, and his hair had been cut.

No, that's not him, I thought.

Still, I kept studying his face—familiar but missing layers of dirt.

Just then, the man saw me. He grinned, raised his hand, waved, and immediately threaded through the vehicles, passing one car and then another at a standstill in all that traffic.

"I didn't recognize you!" I said as he reached my vehicle. "I was worried. Where have you been?"

"In jail."

"What!"

I have come to know this old man very well, and he is the gentlest of souls—completely in his right mind, except for his poverty-driven choices. But he's neither violent nor a criminal.

I didn't realize then that he was about to offer me a valuable Christmas gift, one I will cherish for a lifetime.

How is that possible? How could such a poor soul have anything to give? I will show you.

"Why were you in jail?" I asked.

"A woman called the law on me."

"For what?"

There was no way he had committed a crime. I could feel a protective indignation rising from somewhere deep inside me.

"Trespassing," he said, speaking quietly.

"Trespassing?" I asked, my voice filled with emotion. "You went to jail for trespassing?"

He nodded, but there was no anger in his voice. He didn't seem bitter toward the woman. I, on the other hand, was doing my best not to emit steam.

The incident made me think of a story Jesus told. It seems Peter had come to the Lord and asked how many times he must forgive. Do you recall what Jesus said?

1. Seven times.
2. Seventy times.
3. One hundred times.
4. None of the above.

Review your choices and make your selection.

Here's the Scripture: Peter asked Jesus, "Lord, how many times shall my brother sin against me and I still forgive him? Up to seven times?" Jesus said to him, "I do not say to you, up to seven times, but up to seventy-seven times." [which can also be translated seventy times seven][1]

The correct answer is No. 4, "None of the above."

What Jesus was telling Peter and the disciples was that there's no end to forgiveness. The Lord then immediately reinforced His message with a parable.

Jesus said to His disciples, "For this reason the kingdom of heaven is like a king who wanted to settle accounts with his slaves. And when he had begun to settle them, one who owed him ten thousand talents was brought to him. But since he did not have the means to repay, his master commanded that he be sold, along with his wife and children and all that he had, and repayment be made. So the slave fell to the ground and prostrated himself before him, saying, 'Have patience with me and I will repay you everything.' And the master of that slave felt compassion, and he released him and forgave him the debt."[2]

There is a second slave in this story. Do you recall what happened with his debt?

1. His debt was forgiven.
2. He and his family were sold.
3. He was thrown in prison.
4. None of the above.

Review your choices and make your selection.

Here's the passage: "But that slave [the first who was forgiven] went out and found one of his fellow slaves who owed him a hundred denarii (a much smaller sum); and he seized him and began to choke him, saying, 'Pay back what you owe!' So his fellow slave fell to the ground and began to plead with him, saying, 'Have patience with me and I will repay you.' But he was unwilling, and went and threw him in prison until he would pay back what was owed."[3]

The correct answer is No. 3, "He was thrown in prison."

---

1. Matthew 18:21-22, NASB
2. Matthew 18:23-27, NASB
3. Matthew 18:28-30, NASB

The Lord's parable ends when the angry king discovers what happened and puts the first slave in jail until he repays the debt. Here's the passage:

"Then summoning him, his master said to him, 'You wicked slave, I forgave you all that debt because you pleaded with me. Should you not also have had mercy on your fellow slave, in the same way that I had mercy on you?' And his master, moved with anger, handed him over to the torturers until he would repay all that was owed him."[4]

Jesus ends this parable by telling his disciples firm words. "My heavenly Father will also do the same to you, if each of you does not forgive his brother from your heart."[5]

We think God is all-forgiving, but that's not what Jesus says here. He states that if you don't extend mercy, neither will your heavenly Father offer you mercy. Here it is again:

"My heavenly Father will also do the same to you, if each of you does not forgive his brother from your heart."

It should give you pause.

I'm not telling you what I believe. I am telling you what Jesus said.

And when Jesus taught us to pray, He said these words: "Forgive us our trespasses as we forgive…"[6]

Once again, if you have an unforgiving spirit, aren't you telling God to have that same unforgiving spirit toward you?

Look again at the Lord's Prayer. "Forgive us our trespasses as we forgive…"

The early church repeated the Lord's Prayer three times a day.

David wrote that he praised God seven times a day.[7]

Follow his lead.

Each time, add the Lord's Prayer, repeating Jesus's words: "Forgive us our trespasses as we forgive…"

To secure God's forgiveness, forgive freely.

---

4. Matthew 18:32-34
5. Matthew 18:35, NASB
6. Matthew 6:12, KJV
7. Psalm 119:164, KJV: "Seven times a day do I praise thee because of thy righteous judgments."

This isn't always easy. I will show you more in the third gift of these six: the Gift of Magic. But there's magic in all six of these gifts.

As I said, they changed my life.

Do you see now the old man's sweet Christmas gift? He held nothing hard in his heart toward the woman who had put him in jail.

You can be like that woman, who decided a gentle old man needed to learn a lesson, insisting that he be punished for trespassing. Or you can be like the old man, who forgave her completely.

"Forgive," Jesus said.

Without end, forgive.

Notes, Revelations, Prayers

Date:_____

2. THE GIFT OF HEALING

THIS IS NOT ABOUT SPAGHETTI

"... love the LORD your God, listen to his voice, and hold fast to Him. For the Lord is your life..."

Deuteronomy 30:20[1]

---

1. NIV

THIS IS NOT ABOUT SPAGHETTI

I didn't want any part of it. Spaghetti. Don't get me wrong, Italian food is my favorite. I love pizza, spaghetti, lasagna, eggplant parmesan. I could eat it every day.

But I don't.

I need to eat differently. More fresh food. So, I just walk away.

That's why I didn't want to do it—eat spaghetti. But, get this, the need to eat this pasta kept coming to me. It wasn't a craving; it was a guidance in response to prayer.

"Not good for me, Abba," I said, again and again. But, I'm telling you the truth, God would not let up.

"You can't be serious," I said to Him, day after day. But His guidance was steady. It would not leave me—God does that.

Finally, I surrendered, loading up the sauce with red pepper flakes. I like it spicy. And that changed my world.

What I haven't told you is that six months earlier I had started having pain in my shoulder. It wasn't much at first.

I did some exercises, certain I could work it out.

But, no. The pain increased.

I would sit in church, not able to pay attention, rubbing my shoulder, the pain gnawing at me.

I went to the drugstore, looked for topical pain relievers, and rubbed those into my shoulder. But, no, the pain was deeper.

I used a heating pad. That didn't help either.

Day after day, the pain worsened. I couldn't lift my arm to get dressed. I prayed and prayed for God's help.

I'm a writer, and this was in my right shoulder radiating down my right arm. Severe pain. Intense enough that by two months in, I couldn't write.

In another month, the pain became so severe that I would lie awake at night, unable to sleep. Night after night. I was so tired that it was impossible to accomplish anything.

I didn't want to get a prescription. I don't even take aspirin—my family discouraged the use of pills. Both of my parents said, "If you hurt, your body is trying to tell you something."

Moreover, I thought about people who go to prison, hooked on painkillers and stealing them in the end.

Listen, that can happen to anyone. I hired a nurse to care for my mother when she had cancer, and we discovered she was taking my mom's oxycodone.

Painkiller addiction is real.

Nevertheless, the pain became too much to bear, and I resigned myself to drugs—there was no choice in the matter.

But, through all of this pain and prayer, the Lord kept pointing me to spaghetti. As I said, He would not let up. And it made no sense to me so I fought it, thinking, how can this be from God?

But I've walked with the Lord a long time, and I knew it was. So I gave in. As I said, I loaded up the sauce with red pepper flakes.

Now this is utterly true. The very night after I ate that meal, the pain eased and I slept soundly.

It was nothing short of a miracle!

I had no idea why, but I was determined to find out what spaghetti has to do with pain.

I Googled.

I had just eaten capsaicin, an ingredient in red pepper flakes. It alleviates some types of pain very, very effectively! Who knew?

SIX GIFTS

I put a bottle of those flakes, which cost all of a dollar, in my car, my purse, my kitchen. Then, for a week or so, I sprinkled them on pizza, on salad, on everything. And soon, my pain was completely gone.

A miracle, I tell you! I am so grateful to God!

I've always believed that a cure exists in nature for everything. Immediately, I thought of all those long-ago sailors who died from scurvy.

National Geographic says scurvy causes the body to disintegrate. More than three times as many sailors died from scurvy as all the soldiers killed during the Civil War. It wasn't hundreds of thousands, it was millions who died, and all they needed was an orange. An orange!

A simple cure was found in nature.

It doesn't seem possible. The same with capsaicin. So easy.

But, understand that this chapter is not about spaghetti or cures in nature. What I want you to see is that the Lord is always trying to help you. Listen to Him. Pray and listen.

That awful pain in my shoulder went from the end of 2022 into the spring of 2023. It is now October of 2025 as I revise this book. I occasionally eat red pepper flakes now, just because I like spicy food. But I only needed them a week or so for that pain in my shoulder. It has never returned.

A miracle, I tell you.

And I didn't stumble onto it. All along, God pointed the way!

Pray and listen. Then act on His guidance. ". . . love the Lord your God, listen to his voice, and hold fast to Him. For the Lord is your life…"[1]

---

1. Deuteronomy 30:20, NIV

Notes, Revelations, Prayers

Date:_____

3. THE GIFT OF MAGIC

GOMER PYLE GOD BLESSINGS

"Forgive us our trespasses as we forgive them that trespass against us."

Matthew 6:12[1]

---

1. NMB

GOMER PYLE GOD BLESSINGS

She asked me not to call the police—a college girl driving her grandmother's car. She had been texting when she smashed into me.

I stood on the side of the road in Florida, looking at her and then the damage. I agreed, and we exchanged information. She promised to pay for the repairs.

My mechanic told me what to buy, and he easily fixed my vehicle. I then told her that she didn't owe me anything. I encouraged her to help someone else.

Lucky her? Actually, the lucky one was me.

How so?

A few months later, I backed into a car in my driveway and discovered that I wasn't insured. My new insurance agent wasn't licensed in Florida and hadn't disclosed that. All I could think about was jail time if I had called the police that day, and the police had then discovered that I was paying for insurance in the wrong state. In other words, I was driving uninsured.

Was I grateful to God?

Absolutely.

But I was also angry at my agent.

Moreover, there was a $1,000 premium to get reinsured. I paid it—the agent's wife had cancer, and I didn't want to confront him.

But every time I saw his billboard ad, bitterness swept over me.

As it turns out, I am also quite thankful for my bad agent. From that experience came magic.

Pure, beautiful magic.

I mean it.

Here's how the magic happened.

One day, as I was passing the agent's billboard, the bitter memory of the harm he had caused me returned. But the Lord guided me. God moved me to seek blessings for him.

I thought of Moses, who is one of my heroes in the Bible for that very reason—Moses sought God's forgiveness for wrongdoers who had tried to harm him.

So, I did as I was told.

"God bless you," I said, staring at his billboard. "God bless you. God bless you. God bless you."

I felt as goofy as Gomer Pyle, a character from "Andy Griffith" reruns, who says things over and over again.

But get this—the anger left me!

The next time I passed his sign, the bitterness returned.

"God bless you," I said again. "God bless you. God bless you. God bless you."

And it worked.

Every time I passed that sign, I blessed him again and again, and the anger would leave me.

It was magic!

Months later, I felt overwhelming pain as I learned that a friend had betrayed me. A friend for more than 30 years.

That betrayal did more than just hurt my feelings, it caused me to lose a lot of money.

Bitterness is a hard thing to carry, and then I thought back to that insurance agent and the Gomer-Pyle-style God blessings. Would it work again?

SIX GIFTS

Every time my friend's betrayal came to mind, I said, "God bless you. God bless you. God bless you."

Even if that meant every fifteen minutes.

And it worked. The hurt left me.

Magic, I tell you!

Many say, "Don't retaliate when you're harmed. Walk away and don't look back." But listen to me, if you do that, you will know no one. Your closest and dearest are going to harm you.

Moreover, if you don't deal with the pain, bitterness will grow inside you like a vicious weed. Whenever you recall a painful incident, you'll feel the old bitterness, now bigger.

And that's not good.

It's not healthy.

Countless studies prove that the mind and body are connected. Forgiveness kills the weed of resentment. Forgiveness protects your health.

Then why is it so hard to forgive?

Because forgiveness is unfair. The wrongdoer doesn't deserve to get off. The bad deed should be punished.

As I said, the early church spoke the Lord's Prayer three times a day. Do that every time you pray. When you get to this part, "Forgive me my trespasses as I forgive those who trespass against me," someone may come to mind. Someone who has harmed you.

God bless the person.

Want to forgive, and not just for your health. Simply put, want forgiveness from God. Say to Him, "Forgive me my trespasses as I forgive those who trespass against me."

Want to forgive freely so He will forgive you freely!

Listen carefully, once you learn the power of Gomer-Pyle-style God blessing, you'll forgive easily. You'll also forget.

But is that good?

Are you leaving yourself open for more hurt?

I remember turning to God after another friend betrayed me. "Lord, I forgave and trusted her, and then she harmed me again. What about that?"

Is there an answer in Scripture?

If we eliminate Judas Iscariot from the disciples, whom did Jesus trust?

1. He trusted everyone equally.
2. He trusted the 11 disciples equally.
3. He trusted the 11 disciples, but not equally.
4. The Bible gives no indication.

Think about it a moment.

Now select your answer. Take a guess, even if you aren't sure.

Only three disciples were allowed at certain events—Peter, James, and John.[1]

The answer above is No. 3, "He trusted the 11 disciples, but not equally."

Consider your wounds. Were they from forgiving and forgetting? Or was it because you trusted someone too soon?

Jesus was careful where He placed His trust. Scripture says, "He Himself knew what was in man."[2]

Try out the magic of Gomer-Pyle God blessing today. Live a life of forgiveness.

Say "God bless you, God bless you, God bless you," when you're confronted with a wrongdoer. Believe me, the person most blessed will be you.

---

1. Mark 5:37, ESV: "And he allowed no one to follow him except Peter and James and John the brother of James."

    Mark 9:2, ESV: "After six days Jesus took Peter, James and John with him and led them up a high mountain…"

    Matthew 26:36-38, ESV: "Then Jesus went with them to a place called Gethsemane, and he said to his disciples, 'Sit here, while I go over there and pray.' And taking with him Peter and the two sons of Zebedee, he began to be sorrowful and troubled."

2. John 2:23-25, ESV: "Now when He was in Jerusalem at the Passover Feast, many believed in His name when they saw the signs that He was doing. But Jesus on his part **did not entrust himself to them**, because he knew all people and needed no one to bear witness about man, for He Himself knew what was in man." (Emphasis added)

Notes, Revelations, Prayers

Date:_____

4. THE GIFT OF HOPE

MIRACLES MUST BE REMEMBERED

"Do not forget the things your eyes have seen..."

Deuteronomy 4:9 [1]

---

1. NIV

A BIG FISH TAIL
MIRACLES MUST BE REMEMBERED

There are big-fish tales. You know what I mean, highly unlikely stories—the kind that cause old men to yell, "Balderdash!" This is one of them.

In fact, I wouldn't have the pluck to tell it, but there are witnesses. Living ones.

My big-fish tale began the week before Memorial Day. I wrote about this in *Reaching to God - Joy*, the first volume of the series. I will give you the abridged version here.

My mother's red Cadillac decided to break down near a small town, and the best mechanic there waved me down the road to his mechanic. After a solid week of drama, I switched vehicles and then safely made my long, nearly 1,000-mile trip north in my old Jeep.

There are people—professionals—who say there are no accidents. They insist that one brings disaster upon oneself.

I tend to agree.

Accordingly, I knew who to blame for my next episode of vehicular failure. It didn't help that this mechanic's mechanic had said the Jeep would outlast me, that it could go 900,000 miles with regular service.

That's *not* what happened.

My Jeep died.

Did that occur in any of the many states I had passed through? No. Did it die anywhere on those 1,000 miles of interstate? No. Did it quit near the little town where I had been stranded a week? No, but it did fail.

On June 30, one month after my mom's Cadillac was given last rites, my Jeep died right there, in that same town.

"Balderdash!" you shout.

There are witnesses, I tell you. Living ones!

And the odds. Oh, the odds must be phenomenal.

What are the chances I could ever be stranded again in that same small Southern town, ever in an entire lifetime? Much less twice? Much less with a different vehicle?

As the carnival barker says, "Tighten your belts! This ride gets better!"

Here it is. You don't want to miss this part.

My Jeep didn't break down just anywhere in that town—not on Main Street, not on the highway leading out of town, not even within pushing distance of my automotive mechanic.

Where then?

Every story must have a drumroll, and this is where mine goes. Believe me, it's worth the wait.

My Jeep died at the front door of the automotive repair shop. The front door!

"Balderdash!" you shout.

There are witnesses, I tell you. Living ones!

On that unsuspecting morning, I was headed to see the newspaper editor. I stopped to ask my mechanic a quick question, leaving my Jeep running. As I hurried back toward it, rounding the autos on the lot, the Jeep exploded in a gigantic cloud of steam so thick I couldn't see any part of my vehicle.

Nothing.

At all.

The whole Jeep stood covered in what looked like dense smoke!

The engine died and water gushed to the ground beneath it.

SIX GIFTS

I am telling you this, I wouldn't be penning this now if I had been inside that vehicle—I wouldn't be right for a long time.

I rushed back toward the garage. My mechanic lay full-body in the mouth of a mammoth truck.

"Water—" That was all I could say.

"Was the A/C on?"

He hadn't heard the Jeep and kept working. I stood there, my eyes bulging.

"That's normal," he said.

"Come." I still couldn't talk.

He glanced up at me from the engine. "I can't," he said. "Not right this minute."

But he came immediately, probably because of a look I get—abject horror.

The best-mechanic-in-town's mechanic knew exactly what to do. He opened the hood and reached into the engine. A melon-sized part promptly fell into his hand.

"It's your steering," he said, in a slow drawl.

I stared at the part and swallowed hard—I had felt the steering wheel fighting me.

"It-it-it just started," I stammered, thinking of those folks who say there are no accidents. "I put steering fluid in it. I did!"

That was true—I had, but apparently not soon enough.

He didn't answer me.

Of course, it was my fault, and I wanted to stomp my foot. I should have checked that fluid, but I never do, and nothing like this has ever happened. I rely on oil changes to catch those problems.

Despite this calamity, by nature I am a grateful person. I told the explosion story around town that afternoon, and more than one person lamented my misfortune.

"Good fortune!" I corrected. "I could have been on the interstate. Imagine what might have happened!"

Indeed, several years ago a friend of mine on a motorcycle skidded to a stop on I-65 in the rain. His bike flew out from under him, and he landed on the pavement. A tractor-trailer rolled over his head.

That's a true and tragic story.

It could have been me. Had my Jeep exploded on the interstate, coming to an abrupt halt, a tractor-trailer could have run right over me, crushing my Jeep like a tin can.

There was silence when I returned to see about my Jeep. My mechanic eyed me.

"I know," I said. "I should have checked the steering fluid."

"It wasn't your fault."

"It wasn't?"

"It was a bracket." He stopped, kept looking at me, and shook his head. "A stress fracture."

"What?"

"The odds of that—" He looked away.

Apparently, the odds of a stress fracture were even greater than the odds of it happening in that same small town, with a different vehicle, a month apart, and at his doorstep.

Miracles happen every day. They happen to you and me—our big-fish tales. Is each one the Hand of God guiding and directing us?

I believe so.

Moreover, I strive to hold these moments close. I do that for a very good reason. Why did the Israelites wander for 40 years? Why were the people of God taken into captivity after the grand reign of David?

They lost their faith.

In their fear and suffering, they turned from God. They sought help and guidance elsewhere.

But how did that happen?

How could those chosen by God have forgotten all the miracles Moses showed to Pharaoh—the locusts, the bloody water, the death of every firstborn Egyptian male?

And when they stopped believing in God, how is it that no one shouted, "The Red Sea parted!"?

How could they have left God?

But it happened.

They forgot.

This is one of the saddest themes of the Bible—God's people

SIX GIFTS

forgot what he had done for them and turned away from Him. The verses are too numerous to count. I will add a few in the footnote.[1]

Each of us will go through hard times—one does not get through a lifetime without suffering.

But it is the miracles, the unbelievable moments with God, the times when we see Him gently caring for us, confidently guiding us—they make all the difference.

They embolden us.

They make us raise our eyes to heaven. They remind us to fall to our knees.

Remember the big-fish tales. Remember yours, remember those in the Bible. Boldly tell them to your children, your best friends, and complete strangers.

More importantly, write them down in a book and then read from that book every day.

This is a journal you will want to last a lifetime, so choose a bound book with pages that are sewn and not glued together. Mine is a Moleskine, and it will cost twice the price of a regular glued notebook, but you are only going to buy it once. This is one of the most important items in your walk with God.

Do not neglect writing down your miracles. Add everything you and your family can remember. Date it as best you can. And then be careful to add every new miracle with the date.

I place a topic at the top of the page. I then write that topic in the front of the book with the page number.

You don't need to do that. The most important thing is to faithfully write down every miracle, every intervention of God in your life, as it happens with the date.

And put it in a sewn book so it will not fall apart ten years from now.

Every day, read a miracle.

---

1. Nehemiah 9:13-31
   Psalm 78:5-64
   Ezekiel 33:10-29.

The Hebrews were only three months out of Egypt when they arrived at Mt. Sinai and God gave them His covenant—the Ten Commandments.

It's such a momentous occasion that God descended on the mountaintop before His people in fire and smoke and actually told them the Ten Commandments. They heard Him. [2]

But the Israelites were terrified. They begged Moses to speak to them instead of God. [3]

The rest of the story is well known. Moses went up to the mountaintop, received the tablets of stone with the Ten Commandments, and returned to find the Israelites celebrating. The people thought Moses was not going to return. They had created a golden calf, saying, "These are your gods, O Israel, who brought you up out of the land of Egypt."[4]

Wait. Who?

A golden calf brought them up out of the land of Egypt?

Unbelievable, but it happened. They spoke those words!

There will come times when you will be as overwhelmed as the Israelites. In your fear, you'll think that you cannot trust God.

You'll lose hope.

It happened for centuries across the pages of the Bible. The Israelites had *every* reason to trust God, but they didn't.

If you think you are not like them, you are.

Keep a Miracles Journal

I really cannot stress this enough. Write down what God has done for you. As He gives you new miracles, add to it. Don't say, "I'll never forget." Write it down and read from it every day.

I give you this physical Gift of Hope, which the Lord gave to me.

Big-fish tales from God must be cherished.

The Lord says, "Do not forget the things your eyes have seen."[5]

---

2. Exodus 19:9-20:22
3. Exodus 20:18-22
4. Exodus 32:7-10, ESV
5. Deuteronomy 4:9, NIV

Notes, Revelations, Prayers

Date:_____

5. THE GIFT OF SONG

MY MOM'S MAGIC

"David would take his harp and play it . . . and Saul would be refreshed and be well . . ."

1 SAMUEL 16:23[1]

---

1. NASB(1995)

MY MOM'S MAGIC

"This year," he said. "This coming year, you will be dead." The man wasn't a fortune teller—he was a doctor. An oncologist.

He sat by her hospital bed on Christmas Eve, the night before one of the holiest of Christian holidays. She had been in a car accident, and routine tests had shown Stage-IV breast cancer.

Dr. Jubelirer had never seen her before. She had been brutalized by a tumor that had been misdiagnosed as arthritis, and he had quickly relieved her pain. My mom looked at him with such gratitude. She smiled.

"Do you understand?" he asked in earnest. I think perhaps he moved closer, but I can't remember exactly.

I sat in a chair at the foot of her bed.

"You don't know," I said, my voice filled with belligerence. "You don't."

My dad had died the year before, and my mom was all I had left. I couldn't bear losing her.

He focused on her, explaining her upcoming demise. I think he said he had a "moral obligation" to tell her. I only think that because we heard it so often.

She kept smiling at him, which bewildered the good doctor. But this part was clear to me—my mom was not interested in his predictions. No one told her what to think.

A second specialist appeared the next morning—Christmas Day. They were opening radiation oncology just for her. He told me to call hospice, to get her on the waiting list.

"She'll be dead by February," he said. He had a responsibility to tell us.

We saw more doctors for one reason or another. "You are going to die very soon," each said, making clear their obligation.

She didn't die in February.

Not in March, April, May, or June.

Month after month passed.

I watched as my mom's oncologist gave her the very best care, and I grew to both love and trust Dr. Jubelirer. Accordingly, I began to take that Christmas Eve prediction more seriously.

"Will it be just like a time bomb?" I asked as the next Christmas approached. She seemed much better to me, but I didn't know anything about cancer. "You said a year," I continued. "Will she die without warning?"

He shook his head, saying she was no longer on a death timeline. She was getting better.

But no other doctor agreed with him. We saw a heart specialist when the oncologist detected a murmur.

"She should be dead," the cardiologist announced.

So did the next three and all of the general practitioners. As I said, so many *moral obligations*.

My guess is that most patients would have been at least discouraged, if not depressed. And my mom did almost die—more than once.

Yet her attitude never wavered.

I never saw her feel sorry for herself. Nothing got the best of my mom. Not ever.

She had a great relationship with God, and they had an unspoken secret. She employed God's holy magic in times of distress.

Magic? From God?

What was that?

Honestly, I should have known long before I did.

At the brisk age of two, I was introduced to choir. There were probably seven or eight of us—remember, we were two-year-olds. We had little lemon-colored robes with big red bows at the neck.

"*You* were the choir," my mom said.

According to her, as long as I sang, everyone sang. And when I stopped, everyone stopped.

"You would see a lady's hat," my mom said, "and get distracted."

As my mom told the story, the choir director would quickly wave to me. As soon as I saw him, I was back, bringing along the two-year-olds.

For a decade, choir was my joy, but at twelve I wanted out. That's when I had a rude awakening—choir was not optional. No amount of pleading worked with my mom, not about choir. I had to go.

Like I said, I should have caught on.

As I write this, Christmas morning, I am listening to Handel's *Messiah* and thinking of the last time I was at that concert with her and my father. It was a yearly event at the Municipal Auditorium in my hometown.

When I left for school, as I said earlier, "A Mighty Fortress Is Our God" was always playing.

Do you see a thread here?

Long before scientists proved that music could help stroke patients recover or that music greatly improved motor skills in those with neurological damage, my mom instinctively knew it was potent.

She loved the Gaither specials with their Southern Gospel music, and that became a daily treat during her illness.

The week of Christmas, four years from that fateful Christmas Eve, my mom passed to the Lord.

She never said it, but holy music was her magic. She believed it would get you through when nothing else could. That it could brighten, embolden, and inflate you when something sharp would come your way and try to deflate the ball of life.

Music does just that.

Don't take my word, try it. For a paltry $2.19 when I wrote this in

2015, you could have *Handel's Messiah by the London Philharmonic Choir and Orchestra* as a digital download from Amazon.

The whole thing!

You can put it right on your phone!

Listen to it as you work on your laptop. When I updated *Reaching to God - Joy* in the summer of 2024, I read this chapter for the first time in years. Playing in the background on my laptop was that $2.19 complete version of the *Messiah*!

I find it very comforting.

50 Classic Hymns by various artists and *Come to the Quiet* by John Michael Talbot remain my staple albums.

I like Southern Gospel, but I find joy in a boatload of contemporary Christian music. I can't begin to tell you all the wonderful artists but here is a small preview.

Just about anything by Steven Curtis Chapman is amazing. *8 Greatest Hits* by Phillips, Craig, and Dean; *Welcome to the New* by Mercy Me; "Come Away" and "Rooftops" - Jesus Culture; "Just Say Jesus"- 7eventh Time Down; "Come to the Well," "Thrive," and Until the Whole World Knows" - Casting Crowns; "Steady my Heart" - Kari Jobe; "Love Come to Life" - Big Daddy Weave; "I Need a Miracle" - Third Day; "All the People Said Amen" - Matt Maher; "Live Like That" - Sidewalk Prophets; "By Your Side" - Tenth Avenue North; "Via Dolorosa" - Sandi Patty. There's also Hillsong, and Toby Mac is a great Christian rocker!

Remember, I wrote this list in 2015. Many new and wonderful artists have arrived since then. Don't miss "There Was Jesus," with Zach Williams and Dolly Parton. I could go on and on.

This year, let holy music, a song of praise, lift you, heal you, and brighten your life.

Scripture says, "David would take his harp and play it . . . and Saul would be refreshed and be well . . ."[1]

It's nothing short of magic.

---

1. 1 Samuel 16:23, NASB(1995)

Notes, Revelations, Prayers

Date:_____

6. THE GIFT OF JOY

YOU WILL FIND JOY

"Seven times a day I praise You..."

Psalm 119:164[1]

---

1. NASB

YOU WILL FIND JOY

It happened while she was on the phone with customer service. Mary's cat suddenly ran and hid under her bed, while her little dog jumped beside her, licking her face and demanding attention.

"Just a second, baby," she whispered, rubbing the dog's head and eyeing the cat's path, wondering what was wrong.

"I thought maybe a storm was coming," she told me.

Mary kept trying to straighten out a wrongful billing with a man she couldn't understand.

"I canceled that subscription!" she shouted.

The dog became even more determined to be loved, licking and pawing and nuzzling her.

"I yelled into the phone again," Mary told me, "and my dog became more insistent. That's when I realized there was no one in that room except the three of us—my pets thought I was shouting at them."

"Immediately," Mary told me, "I spoke softly to the man. The cat soon returned, and the dog settled comfortably beside me."

"It was so disrespectful," Mary continued. "I regret speaking that way to anyone."

This is a present-day problem for many. When you call Apple, their recording says to be kind to their customer service people. Apple has wonderful customer service, by the way.

Mary told me she remembered my column about David and the Psalms, how he sang to the Lord. David wrote this:

"Seven times a day I praise You. . ."[1]

In fact, the Psalms are not so much a book as an iPod. They're the songs David lifted to God. Look at the first verses of Psalm 119 and sing them to any tune that comes to mind:

> "Blessed are those whose way is blameless,
> Who walk in the Law of the Lord.
> Blessed are those who comply with His testimonies,
> And seek Him with all their heart."[2]

See, with music it has a very different impact.

Ask yourself, when did David start praising the Lord seven times a day? Was it during his stressful days as an army commander[3] or his years as a shepherd boy?

David pointedly told Saul that his young life hadn't been one surrounded by the peaceful bleating of lambs. Rather, he had rescued sheep from the mouths of lions and bears.[4]

Rough work!

We don't know when David began his practice of praise, but we do know he was a musician for King Saul.[5]

You may be thinking that you can't praise God seven times a day—you have a job, children. But how did David do it?

Can you imagine?

---

1. Psalm 119:164, NASB
2. Psalm 119:1-2, NASB
3. 1 Samuel 18:5-7
4. 1 Samuel 17:34-36, NIV: "But David said to Saul, 'Your servant has been keeping his father's sheep. When a lion or a bear came and carried off a sheep from the flock, I went after it, struck it and rescued the sheep from its mouth. When it turned on me, I seized it by its hair, struck it and killed it. Your servant has killed both the lion and the bear...'"
5. 1 Samuel 16:14-23

SIX GIFTS

He wasn't just a shepherd, a musician, and a general. Remember that David was then a fugitive running for his life. "Now Saul told his son Jonathan and all his servants to put David to death."[6]

David fled, 400 men joined him, and he became their captain. Believe me, that was an even rougher time.[7]

After King Saul died, David didn't finally have rest. He fought a civil war with Saul's son for years.[8]

Once that war ended, David had Israel's enemies to defeat and then a nation to lead. So, how did he make it work?

Did David leave battles or meetings with his military commanders to praise God? If his troops were marching along, did he take a time out and retire somewhere to sing? What about when he was living in his palace, with the hustle and bustle of everyone needing him?

Again, how did David make it work?

How would you have advised David?

To praise God alongside those soldiers and sing with all in the palace? If you had been in charge, wouldn't that have been your practice?

It still can be.

You can lead your family, your employees, your boss in a song of praise. You can set the clock on your phone to turn on music and to say, "David praised God seven times a day."

Not only will it get the praise times in, but you will begin to say, "If David can do it, I can do it."

Honestly, this was not an easy change for me. I slip into "a flow" when I write, and I lose all track of time and place.

I always felt like that flow was a gift from God. When my phone would sound, calling me to praise, I turned it off. Staying in the flow was more important.

But the Lord showed me that I was wrong. Each time I praised Him and also said the Lord's Prayer, it was a shot of power and guidance.

---

6. 1 Samuel 19:1, NASB
7. 1 Samuel 22:2
8. 2 Samuel 1:1-5:5

True.

Yet you have to be careful about anything you do repeatedly. Be on the watch for it becoming meaningless, just rotely saying the words.

Talk to God with each section of the Lord's Prayer. When you say "hallowed be Thy name," pause to speak more with Him. When you say, "Thy kingdom come, Thy will be done, on earth as it is in heaven," pause again. The same after, "Give me this day my daily bread." And so on, praying more in depth about the words you have just said.

You may also want to do as Brother Lawrence did, see yourself with God in heaven. The monk wrote about this in his letters, which were compiled and became "Practice of the Presence of God."

The book was assigned reading in seminary. It's a deceptively simple text but considered a classic of Christian devotion. "He [Brother Lawrence] considered himself as a subject before his King, or as a son before his father... he was sometimes as it were embraced by Him... treated him as his favourite." [9]

It gets better.

We all have ways we disappoint the Lord—lying, anger, selfishness. The list of vices differs for each of us.

"I didn't think I could ever become patient," Mary said. "Now, by the time I get at rip-roaring speed, my phone comes on and calls me to praise. It's like putting the brakes to an out-of-control vehicle. Once I have praised Him and said the Lord's prayer, I am changed."

David's seven times of praise and the early church's commitment to the Lord's Prayer will change you, too. You'll wake up singing, go to bed singing, sing in your sleep.

Your drawn face and wrinkles will soften. Your focus will sharpen. You will accomplish what you long to do.

There's more. It gets even better.

You will find joy.

---

9. *Practice of the Presence of God* by Brother Lawrence (Nicholas Herman), Classic Translation, 1800s

Notes, Revelations, Prayers

Date:_____

THE LIGHT

"I am the Light of the world."

John 9:5[1]

---

1. NASB

REJECTED GIFTS

MUD PIES & SQUASHED SANDWICHES

"And He could not do any miracle there except that He laid His hands on a few sick people and healed them. And He was amazed at their unbelief."

Mark 6:5-6[1]

---

1. NASB

MUD PIES & SQUASHED SANDWICHES

One sunny morning, I spotted the man who lives under the bridge as he stood on his regular street corner.

As I said earlier, he's gentle. But don't get me wrong—he's also earnest with his panhandling sign. He's there for a reason.

Some days, that makes me laugh. This was one of those days.

There was no traffic, so I was able to pull beside him and stop.

"Do you like peanut butter?" I asked.

"Yes." He grinned, looking inside my vehicle.

I reached for the sandwich I had made for myself. It was a sacrifice—I was traveling and needed it. Even so, I didn't want him to go hungry and didn't have time to find him something.

I handed it through the window, and he shook his head.

"No," he said.

"It's good. Peanut butter and homemade jam on Ezekiel bread."

"No," he said, this time firmly, stepping back from my car.

"But you said you liked peanut butter."

"I don't like that kind."

Okay, I laughed. What I haven't told you is that the sandwich didn't look exactly right—I had sat on half of it.

But I kept trying.

"Honestly, it's good," I said. "It just looks a little—"

He eyed the squashed side.

I turned the good side to him.

"No," he said, walking away.

So, I gave up and left. But I thought of him later while eating that great sandwich. The disfigured side didn't make it any less delicious.

It made me think of Jesus and the nameless blind man. When Jesus encountered that blind man, the Lord spit on the ground and placed mud on the man's eyes.

What did Jesus say?

The Lord said, "I am the Light of the world."

Here's the passage:

"As Jesus passed by, He saw a man who had been blind from birth . . . [and said] 'I am the Light of the world.' When He had said this, He spit on the ground, and made mud from the saliva, and applied the mud to his eyes and said to him, 'Go, wash in the pool of Siloam' (which is translated, 'Sent')..."[1]

How did the blind man respond?

Now remember, he has mud on his eyes made from Jesus's spit. The man wasn't deaf—he knew where it came from.

Did the blind man walk away, disgusted?

Or did he ask Jesus to come with him, not certain the mud would really work?

Here's the rest of the passage: ". . . and [Jesus] said to him, 'Go, wash in the pool of Siloam' ... So, he left and washed, and came back seeing."[2]

The blind man hadn't asked Jesus anything. He simply believed.

Jesus's healings didn't always go like that. Remember blind Bartimaeus? He received a much better deal.

Here's the passage:

". . . as [Jesus] was leaving Jericho . . . a beggar who was blind named Bartimaeus . . . began to cry out . . . And Jesus said to him, 'Go;

---

1. John 9:1-7, NASB
2. John 9:7, NASB

your faith has made you well.' And immediately he regained his sight . . ."[3] [4]

In other words, Bartimaeus didn't have to deal with spit or mud pies. He didn't have to be led to a pool to wash to find out his fate.

No, Bartimaeus was healed at once!

But everyone who saw Jesus and needed healing had faith, right? Hardly.

Recall when Jesus was teaching in His hometown of Nazareth? Here it is:

"Jesus . . . came into His hometown . . . began to teach . . . and the many listeners were astonished, saying, 'Where did this man learn these things, and what is this wisdom . . . Is this not the carpenter . . . And they took offense at Him.'"[5]

The people of Nazareth thought Jesus was acting bigger than His britches. Scripture says, "And He could not do any miracle there except that He laid His hands on a few sick people and healed them. And He was amazed at their unbelief."[6]

The nameless blind man took no offense at Jesus's spit or the mud on his eyes. Instead, he and his dirty face went and washed without asking anything.

He had what the people of Nazareth did not. He had blind faith!

God has handed me many ugly sandwiches and wiped my eyes with mud pies. He's led me down paths I didn't want to walk, guided me on journeys that couldn't possibly be right.

But God knew what He was up to.

A woman recently asked me, "What will you be doing in five years?"

I mentioned that to my friend of thirty years, Teri Youhanaie.

---

3. Mark 10:46-52, NASB
4. Understand that I left out most of the story and focused on one point: Jesus said that Bartimaeus's faith had made him well. Read the whole passage, when you get a chance, and the chapter devoted to Bartimaeus in *Reaching to God, Joy,* the first volume of the *Reaching to God* series, because there's more you won't want to miss. It's an inspiring story about perseverance.
5. Mark 6:1-3, NASB
6. Mark 6:5-6, NASB

"I didn't know what to say to her, Teri."

"That's easy," she answered. "What you're doing right now."

It's true. I really love everything God has given to me. But, at the outset, I didn't want to become a faith columnist or a lawyer. The Lord pushed me into both.

Prayer is answered differently for different people. Yours might come immediately, as it did for Bartimaeus, or in a muddy mess, as it did for the first blind man.

You may get answers that you don't want.

The old panhandler didn't want my sandwich, but he missed out. God isn't always going to give you what "looks right."

This isn't just about presents on Christmas Day. God is looking for ways to bless you all the time. And the best of His gifts may appear as mud pies and squashed sandwiches.

Don't turn away.

When the Lord speaks to you, whatever you're guided to do, follow Him. Follow Him blindly.

Jesus is the Light for your world.

Thank you for letting me share my faith with you this Christmas.
Stay close to God.

Notes, Revelations, Prayers

Date:_____

THE CHRISTMAS QUIZ ANSWERS

"May the God of hope fill you with all joy and peace in believing, so that by the power of the Holy Spirit you may abound in hope."

Romans 15:13[1]

---

1. ESV

REVISITING THE TWO YOUNG MECHANICS

Remember that cold day and the two mechanics in the gas station waiting area? They proudly finished my quiz, pleased with their score, and went back to work.

Here are the answers.

Question 1

What happened 15 months before the birth of Jesus that kicks off the Christmas story?
1. The angel Gabriel speaks to Mary.
2. The angel Gabriel speaks to a priest.
3. An angel appears in a dream to Joseph.
4. All of the above

Consider the answers carefully and make your choice.

Here is the passage: "In the days of Herod, king of Judea, there was a priest named Zechariah . . . righteous in the sight of God . . . Now an angel of the Lord appeared to him ... and said, 'I am Gabriel.'"[1]

The angel tells the priest that he will have a son and to name him

---

1. Luke 1:5-19, NASB

"John." Gabriel says, "He will bring back many of the people of Israel to the Lord their God."[2] This is John the Baptist.

The answer is No. 2, Gabriel speaks to a priest.

Question 2

When the angel Gabriel spoke to Mary, telling her she would give birth, what else did Gabriel say to her?
1. To name her son Jesus
2. That the baby would be the Son of God
3. That the Holy Spirit would come upon her
4. All of the above

Consider the answers carefully and make your choice.

Here's the passage: "And the angel said to [Mary], 'Do not be afraid, Mary, for you have found favor with God. And behold, you will conceive in your womb and give birth to a son, and you shall name Him Jesus . . . The Holy Spirit will come upon you, and the power of the Most High will overshadow you; for that reason also the holy Child will be called the Son of God.'"[3]

The answer is No. 4, all of the above.

That was a hard one. I couldn't remember if Mary knew from the beginning that Jesus would be the Son of God. But she did.

Question 3

According to Scripture, after Gabriel appeared to Mary, how did she feel and what did she decide to do first?
1. She was afraid and only told Joseph.
2. She was confused and spent time alone in prayer.
3. She hurried south and spent three joyous months with relatives.
4. None of the above.

Consider your answers carefully and make your choice.

---

2. Luke 1:16, NIV
3. Luke 1:30-35, ESV

THE CHRISTMAS QUIZ ANSWERS

After Gabriel appears to Mary, she goes and stays with her relatives, the priest Zechariah and his wife Elizabeth, where she celebrates her good fortune.

Here's the passage: Gabriel tells Mary, "'And behold, even your relative Elizabeth herself has conceived a son in her old age, and she who was called infertile is now in her sixth month' . . . And the angel departed from her.

"Now at this time Mary set out and went in a hurry to the hill country, to a city of Judah, and she entered the house of Zechariah and greeted Elizabeth . . . And Mary said: 'My soul exalts the Lord, And my spirit has rejoiced in God my Savior.'"[4]

The answer is No. 3, "She hurried south and joyously spent three months with relatives."

Question 4

Why did Mary and Joseph suddenly travel to Bethlehem when Mary was nine months pregnant?

1. Herod had ordered them to move.
2. Caesar Augustus had ordered a count of his kingdom.
3. Julius Caesar wanted to tax all the inhabitants of Rome.
4. The angel Gabriel told them to go.

Consider your answers carefully and make your choice.

Here's the passage:

"Now in those days a decree went out from Caesar Augustus, that a census be taken of all the inhabited earth . . . Now Joseph also went up from Galilee, from the city of Nazareth, to Judea, to the city of David which is called Bethlehem ... along with Mary ..." [5]

The answer is No. 2, the decree put in the mind of Caesar Augustus by God to fulfill His prophecy.

---

4. Luke 1:39-47, NASB
5. Luke 2:1-5, NASB

Question 5

According to Scripture, Magi came from the East to see Jesus and stopped first in Jerusalem. When they asked where they could find the newborn King of the Jews, what happened in the city:

1. Everyone rejoiced and awaited their return.
2. Everyone was troubled.
3. Everyone followed the Magi to Bethlehem.
4. None of the above

Consider your answers carefully and make your choice.

Here is the passage: "Now after Jesus was born in Bethlehem of Judea in the days of Herod the king, behold, magi from the east arrived in Jerusalem, saying, 'Where is He who has been born King of the Jews? For we saw His star in the east and have come to worship Him.' When Herod the king heard this, he was troubled, and all Jerusalem with him."[6]

The answer is No. 2, "Everyone was troubled."

Question 6

Following the Law of Moses, Jesus was presented at the temple forty days after His birth, and a sacrifice was offered. Who did Mary and Joseph meet when they were at the temple?

1. Herod the Great and his soldiers
2. Simeon, a righteous man, and Anna, the prophetess
3. The Apostle Paul
4. John the Baptist

Consider your answers carefully and make your choice.

Here's the passage: "And there was a man in Jerusalem whose name was Simeon; and this man was righteous and devout . . . [and] he took [Jesus] in his arms, and blessed God, and said, 'Now, Lord, You are letting Your bond-servant depart in peace . . . For my eyes have seen Your salvation" . . . And there was a prophetess, Anna, . . . And

---

6. Matthew 2:1-3, NASB

at that very moment she came up and began giving thanks to God, and continued to speak about Him to all those who were looking forward to the redemption of Jerusalem."[7]

The answer is No. 2, Simeon, a righteous man, and Anna, the prophetess.

Question 7

Herod the Great killed all the male infants in and around Bethlehem. He lived during the Civil War in Rome. Did he side with:

1. Octavian, who became Caesar Augustus, and Marc Antony
2. Cleopatra and Pharaoh
3. Julius Caesar
4. Pontius Pilate
5. None of the above

Consider your answers carefully and make your choice.

This passage is not in Scripture. But learning the history before the birth of Jesus is truly helpful in understanding Herod the Great and the fear in the people of Jerusalem.

The answer is No. 5, None of the above. Herod sided with Marc Antony and Cleopatra against Octavian.

Question 8

Luke does not include the Magi in his Gospel, but he does tell us a huge clue as to when the Magi arrived. What is that little detail, nearly hidden in the Christmas story?

1. Jesus wore a gold ring when He was presented at the temple.
2. Mary and Joseph told Simeon about the Magi.
3. Simeon said he had seen the Magi.
4. Mary and Joseph offered turtledoves or young doves when Jesus was presented.

Consider your choices and select your answer.

---

7. Luke 2:25-38, NASB

Here's the passage: "And when the days for their purification according to the Law of Moses were completed, they brought Him up to Jerusalem to present Him to the Lord (as it is written in the Law of the Lord: 'Every firstborn male that opens the womb shall be called holy to the Lord'), and to offer a sacrifice according to what has been stated in the Law of the Lord: 'A pair of turtledoves or two young doves.'"[8]

That was the offering of the poor.[9]

If the Magi had come, Mary and Joseph would have been able to offer a lamb. The Magi would have brought presents of great wealth, fit for the king they had traveled so far to worship.

The correct answer is No. 4. "Mary and Joseph offered turtledoves or young doves when Jesus was presented."

Question 9

According to Scripture, how many Magi came from the East to see Jesus?

1. One
2. Three
3. One hundred
4. None of the above

Consider your choices and lock in your answer.

This one is difficult to remember given all the Christmas cards, nativity scenes, and ads with three Magi. The answer is No. 4, None of the above. Scripture is silent on the number.

A Joy-Filled Moment

I couldn't take my eyes off those two mechanics, listening to them talk through Scripture they knew, narrowing the choices.

Why?

---

8. Luke 2:22-24, NASB
9. Leviticus 14:21-22

THE CHRISTMAS QUIZ ANSWERS

Because they could have spent their break doing anything. Instead, they wanted to read about the Christmas story.

I graduated from the highest-ranked Baptist Seminary in the world, and there were only seven women in my class. I had to fight to get in.

If you weren't going into missions, you were told that it was a waste of everyone's time, that you'd never find work.

I'm also ordained.

Ordination is a careful process. The candidate writes a paper on his or her theology and is then examined by a board of ministers. They recommended me.

Then you meet and speak before all of the pastors in the churches in your association. Each church usually sends two representatives.

I had been told that the President of the Association had made it clear that every man needed to attend to vote against me. There was only one woman eligible to attend.

They listened to me, and the Holy Spirit touched their hearts. I was approved for ordination not just by one Baptist church, but by the Association of Baptist Churches to which my church belongs.

And this was south of the Mason-Dixon Line.

I only tell you because I didn't do any of it on my own—the Lord decided. He made the impossible possible; removing walls, changing the hearts of men determined to block me, educating me with professors who had the best minds in theology, ordaining me to share His words, and giving me a path.

When I have the opportunity to draw a person into a closer relationship with Him, that's as good as it gets. My calling. So, that moment in 2016, with those two mechanics, filled me with great joy.

My eyes glaze with tears of gratitude as I tell you my journey, remembering the Lord's Presence with me all along the way.

The impossible made possible.

Notes, Revelations, Prayers

Date:_____

Notes, Revelations, Prayers

Date:_____

ALSO BY R.A. MATHEWS

I. Non-Fiction Available Now

Vol. 1 Reaching to God, Joy: The Joy of His Presence

Vol. 2 Reaching to God, Hope: The Hope of the Ages

Vol. 3 Reaching to God, The Christmas Edition

II. Non-Fiction Upcoming Releases

Vol. 4 Reaching to God, Love: His Love Endures Forever

Vol. 5 Reaching to God, Faith

Vol. 6 Reaching to God, The Angels Edition

III. Fiction Available Now

Missing Jogger

by I.C. Ford

(one of her two pen names)

IV. You Can Read Free!

Every week, you can read a free faith article by R.A. Mathews.

Just ask the Editor or Features Editor at your newspaper to contact us, and we'll send your local newspaper a complimentary column every week. Then read free!

Make that call, send an email, or, if it's a small paper, stop by your newspaper with your book. Do it today. Talk to your newspaper editor. He or she is in the business of selling papers and wants to hear from you.

REACHING TO God
JOY
Volume 1

R.A. MATHEWS

BIBLE YOU DIDN'T KNOW
STORIES TO STRENGTHEN THE SOUL

REACHING TO God
HOPE
Volume 2

R.A. MATHEWS

BIBLE YOU DIDN'T KNOW
STORIES TO STRENGTHEN THE SOUL

ACKNOWLEDGMENTS

Edited by **Teresa Zintgraff Youhanaie**

It is a pleasure to have many to thank for this book. I am grateful for the presence of each of you in my life.

To **Brenda Shoffner**, my longtime editor at the Northwest Florida Daily News: Every week, I learned from your vast knowledge. I will never forget you and always be grateful!

To **Jimmy Parsons**, my dear friend's *Gp*, Grandpa, and my *Gp*, Godpaw. The Lord offers heavenly beings to guide and protect us. He will also offer souls on earth to be His right hand, Godpaw.

Thank you, **Gp**, for being such a witness for the Lord and for always encouraging me!

To my first newspaper editors, **Josh Richards** and **Jay Thomas**: This book would not have flourished had you each not believed in me and kept publishing my thoughts. Thank you!

To **Preston Boutwell**, who made Bobby run and get a newspaper and then shoved it at me, insisting I write something: Thank you. The Lord was in that moment!

My thanks to **David Ellis**, who kept me from leaving my great little town with its newspaper that wanted me. You brought me back to the house I adore again and again.

I want to extend great love and appreciation to **Jacqueline Turley, Melanie Ezell, Karin Patton**, and **Jane Charnock**. You have my heartfelt thanks! You each gave generously of your time to comment and guide me. Thank you!

CHRISTMAS SCRIPTURE

MATTHEW'S GOSPEL
MATTHEW CHAPTERS 1 - 2, NASB

The Genealogy of Jesus the Messiah

1 The [a]record of the genealogy of [b]Jesus the [c]Messiah, the son of David, the son of Abraham:
2 Abraham fathered Isaac, Isaac fathered Jacob, and Jacob fathered [d]Judah and his brothers. 3 Judah fathered Perez and Zerah by Tamar, Perez fathered Hezron, and Hezron fathered [e]Ram. 4 Ram fathered Amminadab, Amminadab fathered Nahshon, and Nahshon fathered Salmon. 5 Salmon fathered Boaz by Rahab, Boaz fathered Obed by Ruth, and Obed fathered Jesse. 6 Jesse fathered David the king.
David fathered Solomon by [f]her *who had been the wife* of Uriah. 7 Solomon fathered Rehoboam, Rehoboam fathered Abijah, and Abijah fathered [g]Asa. 8 Asa fathered Jehoshaphat, Jehoshaphat fathered [h]Joram, and Joram fathered Uzziah. 9 Uzziah fathered [i]Jotham, Jotham fathered Ahaz, and Ahaz fathered Hezekiah. 10 Hezekiah fathered Manasseh, Manasseh fathered [j]Amon, and Amon fathered Josiah. 11 Josiah fathered [k]Jeconiah and his brothers, at the time of the deportation to Babylon.
12 After the deportation to Babylon: Jeconiah fathered [l]Shealtiel, and Shealtiel fathered Zerubbabel. 13 Zerubbabel fathered [m]Abihud,

Abihud fathered Eliakim, and Eliakim fathered Azor. **14** Azor fathered Zadok, Zadok fathered Achim, and Achim fathered Eliud. **15** Eliud fathered Eleazar, Eleazar fathered Matthan, and Matthan fathered Jacob. **16** Jacob fathered Joseph the husband of Mary, by whom Jesus was born, who is called the [n]Messiah.

17 So all the generations from Abraham to David are fourteen generations; from David to the deportation to Babylon, fourteen generations; and from the deportation to Babylon to the [o]Messiah, fourteen generations.

Conception and Birth of Jesus

18 Now the birth of Jesus the [p]Messiah was as follows: when His mother Mary had been [q]betrothed to Joseph, before they came together she was found to be pregnant by the Holy Spirit. **19** And her husband Joseph, since he was a righteous man and did not want to disgrace her, planned to [r]send her away secretly. **20** But when he had thought this over, behold, an angel of the Lord appeared to him in a dream, saying, "Joseph, son of David, do not be afraid to take Mary as your wife; for [s]the Child who has been conceived in her is of the Holy Spirit. **21** She will give birth to a Son; and you shall name Him Jesus, for [t]He will save His people from their sins." **22** Now all this [u]took place so that what was spoken by the Lord through [v]the prophet would be fulfilled: **23** "Behold, the virgin will [w]conceive and give birth to a Son, and they shall name Him [x]Immanuel," which translated means, "God with us." **24** And Joseph awoke from his sleep and did as the angel of the Lord commanded him, and took *Mary* as his wife, **25** [y]but kept her a virgin until she gave birth to a Son; and he named Him Jesus.

The Visit of the Magi

Chapter 2 1 Now after Jesus was born in Bethlehem of Judea in the days of Herod the king, behold, [z]magi from the east arrived in Jerusalem, saying, **2** "Where is He who has been born King of the

Jews? For we saw His star in the east and have come to worship Him."
3 When Herod the king heard *this*, he was troubled, and all Jerusalem with him. **4** And gathering together all the chief priests and scribes of the people, he inquired of them where the [aa]Messiah was to be born. **5** They said to him, "In Bethlehem of Judea; for this is what has been written [ab]by [ac]the prophet:

6

'And you, Bethlehem, land of Judah,
Are by no means least among the leaders of Judah;
For from you will come forth a Ruler
Who will shepherd My people Israel.'"

7 Then Herod secretly called for the magi and determined from them the exact [ad]time the star appeared. **8** And he sent them to Bethlehem and said, "Go and search carefully for the Child; and when you have found *Him*, report to me, so that I too may come and worship Him." **9** After hearing the king, they went on their way; and behold, the star, which they had seen in the east, went on ahead of them until it came to a stop over *the place* where the Child was *to be found*. **10** When they saw the star, they rejoiced exceedingly with great joy. **11** And after they came into the house, they saw the Child with His mother Mary; and they fell down and [ae]worshiped Him. Then they opened their treasures and presented to Him gifts of gold, frankincense, and myrrh. **12** And after being warned *by God* in a dream not to return to Herod, *the magi* left for their own country by another way.

The Escape to Egypt

13 Now when they had gone, behold, an angel of the Lord *appeared to Joseph in a dream and said, "Get up! Take the Child and His mother and flee to Egypt, and stay there until I tell you; for Herod is going to search for the Child to kill Him."
14 So [af]Joseph got up and took the Child and His mother while it was still night, and left for Egypt. **15** He [ag]stayed there until the death of Herod; *this happened* so that what had been spoken by the

Lord through [ah]the prophet would be fulfilled: "Out of Egypt I called My Son."

Herod Slaughters Babies

16 Then when Herod saw that he had been tricked by the magi, he became very enraged, and sent *men* and killed all the boys who were in Bethlehem and all its vicinity [ai]who were two years old or under, according to the time which he had determined from the magi. **17** Then what had been spoken through Jeremiah the prophet was fulfilled:
18
"A voice was heard in Ramah,
Weeping and great mourning,
Rachel weeping for her children;
And she refused to be comforted,
Because they were no more."

19 But when Herod died, behold, an angel of the Lord *appeared in a dream to Joseph in Egypt, and said, **20** "Get up, take the Child and His mother, and go to the land of Israel; for those who sought the Child's life are dead." **21** So [aj]Joseph got up, took the Child and His mother, and came into the land of Israel. **22** But when he heard that Archelaus was reigning over Judea in place of his father Herod, he was afraid to go there. Then after being warned *by God* in a dream, he left for the regions of Galilee, **23** and came and settled in a city called Nazareth. *This happened* so that what was spoken through the prophets would be fulfilled: "He will be called a Nazarene."

Footnotes

a Matthew 1:1 Lit *book*

b Matthew 1:1 In Heb *Yeshua (Joshua)*, meaning *The Lord is salvation*

c Matthew 1:1 From Gr *Christos*, which means *Messiah* (Heb for Anointed One)

d Matthew 1:2 Gr *Judas*; a name of a person in the Old Testament is given in its Old Testament form

CHRISTMAS SCRIPTURE

e Matthew 1:3 Gr *Aram*
f Matthew 1:6 I.e., Bathsheba
g Matthew 1:7 Gr *Asaph*
h Matthew 1:8 Also Gr for *Jehoram* in 2 Kin 8:16; cf. 1 Chr 3:11
i Matthew 1:9 Gr *Joatham*
j Matthew 1:10 Gr *Amos*
k Matthew 1:11 *Jehoiachin* in 2 Kin 24:15
l Matthew 1:12 Gr *Salathiel*
m Matthew 1:13 Gr *Abioud*, usually spelled *Abiud*
n Matthew 1:16 From Gr *Christos*, which means *Messiah* (Heb for Anointed One)
o Matthew 1:17 See note v 16
p Matthew 1:18 See note v 16
q Matthew 1:18 Unlike engagement, a betrothed couple was considered married, but did not yet live together
r Matthew 1:19 Or *divorce her*
s Matthew 1:20 Lit *that which*
t Matthew 1:21 Lit *He Himself*
u Matthew 1:22 Lit *has happened*
v Matthew 1:22 I.e., Isaiah
w Matthew 1:23 Or *be pregnant*
x Matthew 1:23 Gr *Emmanuel*
y Matthew 1:25 Lit *and did not know her* intimately
z Matthew 2:1 A caste of educated men specializing in astronomy, astrology, and natural science
a Matthew 2:4 From Gr *Christos*, which means *Messiah* (Heb for Anointed One)
b Matthew 2:5 Or *through*
c Matthew 2:5 I.e., Micah
d Matthew 2:7 Lit *time of the appearing star*
e Matthew 2:11 Lit *prostrated themselves to*; i.e., lay face down in a prone position to indicate worship
f Matthew 2:14 Lit *he*
g Matthew 2:15 Lit *was*

h [Matthew 2:15](#) I.e., Hosea
i [Matthew 2:16](#) Lit *from two...and under*
j [Matthew 2:21](#) Lit *he*

LUKE'S GOSPEL
LUKE 1:1 - 2:40, NASB

Luke Writes to Most Excellent Theophilus

1 Since many have undertaken to compile an account of the things [a]accomplished among us, 2 just as they were handed down to us by those who from the beginning [b]were eyewitnesses and [c]servants of the [d]word, 3 it seemed fitting to me as well, having [e]investigated everything carefully from the beginning, to write *it out* for you in an orderly sequence, most excellent Theophilus; 4 so that you may know the exact truth about the [f]things you have been [g]taught.

The Priest Zechariah

5 In the days of Herod, king of Judea, there was a priest named Zechariah, of the division of [h]Abijah; and he had a wife [i]from the daughters of Aaron, and her name was Elizabeth. 6 They were both righteous in the sight of God, walking blamelessly in all the commandments and requirements of the Lord. 7 And *yet* they had no child, because Elizabeth was infertile, and they were both advanced in [j]years.

8 Now it happened *that* while he was performing his priestly

service before God in the appointed order of his division, **9** according to the custom of the priestly office, he was chosen by lot to enter the temple of the Lord and burn incense. **10** And the whole multitude of the people were in prayer outside at the hour of the incense offering.

The Angel Gabriel Appears to Zechariah Saying He Will Have a Son, John the Baptist

11 Now an angel of the Lord appeared to him, standing to the right of the altar of incense. **12** Zechariah was troubled when he saw *the angel*, and fear [k]gripped him. **13** But the angel said to him, "Do not be afraid, Zechariah, for your prayer has been heard, and your wife Elizabeth will bear you a son, and you shall [l]name him John. **14** You will have joy and gladness, and many will rejoice over his birth. **15** For he will be great in the sight of the Lord; and he will drink no wine or liquor, and he will be filled with the Holy Spirit [m]while still in his mother's womb. **16** And he will turn many of the sons of Israel back to the Lord their God. **17** And *it is* he *who* will go *as a forerunner* before Him in the spirit and power of Elijah, to turn the hearts of fathers back to *their* children, and the disobedient to the attitude of the righteous, to make ready a people prepared for the Lord."

Zechariah Doubts Gabriel

18 Zechariah said to the angel, "How will I know this? For I am an old man, and my wife is advanced in her [n]years." **19** The angel answered and said to him, "I am Gabriel, who [o]stands in the presence of God, and I was sent to speak to you and to bring you this good news.

Zechariah Struck Mute by Gabriel

20 And behold, you will be silent and unable to speak until the day when these things take place, because you did not believe my words, which will be fulfilled at their proper time."

21 And *meanwhile* the people were waiting for Zechariah, and were wondering at his delay in the temple. **22** But when he came out, he was unable to speak to them; and they realized that he had seen a vision in the temple, and he *repeatedly* [p]made signs to them, and remained speechless. **23** When the days of his priestly service were concluded, he went back home.

Zechariah's Wife Elizabeth Secludes Herself for Five Months

24 Now after these days his wife Elizabeth became pregnant, and she kept herself [q]in seclusion for five months, saying, **25** "This is the way the Lord has dealt with me in the days when He looked *with favor* upon *me*, to take away my disgrace among people."

Gabriel Visits the Virgin Mary
Announcing the Birth of Jesus

26 Now in the sixth month the angel Gabriel was sent from God to a city in Galilee named Nazareth, **27** to a virgin [r]betrothed to a man whose name was Joseph, of the [s]descendants of David; and the virgin's name was [t]Mary. **28** And coming in, he said to her, "Greetings, favored one! The Lord [u]*is* with you." **29** But she was very perplexed at *this* statement, and was pondering what kind of greeting this was. **30** And the angel said to her, "Do not be afraid, Mary, for you have found favor with God. **31** And behold, you will conceive in your womb and give birth to a son, and you shall name Him Jesus. **32** He will be great and will be called the Son of the Most High; and the Lord God will give Him the throne of His father David; **33** and He will reign over the house of Jacob forever, and His kingdom will have no end." **34** But Mary said to the angel, "How will this be, since I [v]am a virgin?" **35** The angel answered and said to her, "The Holy Spirit will come upon you, and the power of the Most High will overshadow you; for that reason also the [w]holy Child will be called the Son of God. **36** And behold, even your relative Elizabeth herself has conceived a son in her old age, and [x]she who was called infertile is now in her sixth month. **37** For nothing will be impossible with God." **38** And Mary said, "Behold, the Lord's bond-servant; may it be done to me according to your word." And the angel departed from her.

Mary and Elizabeth Celebrate

39 Now [y]at this time Mary set out and went in a hurry to the hill country, to a city of Judah, **40** and she entered the house of Zechariah and greeted Elizabeth. **41** When Elizabeth heard Mary's greeting, the baby leaped in her womb, and Elizabeth was filled with the Holy Spirit. **42** And she cried out with a loud voice and said, "Blessed *are* you among women, and blessed *is* the fruit of your womb! **43** And [z]how has it happened to me that the mother of my Lord would come to me? **44** For behold, when the sound of your greeting reached my ears, the baby leaped in my womb for joy. **45** And blessed *is* she who [aa]believed that there would be a fulfillment of what had been spoken to her [ab]by the Lord."

Mary Rejoices

46 And Mary said:
"My soul [ac]exalts the Lord,
47
And my spirit has rejoiced in God my Savior.
48
For He has had regard for the humble state of His bond-servant;
For behold, from now *on* all generations will [ad]call me blessed.
49
For the Mighty One has done great things for me;
And holy is His name.
50
And His mercy is to generation [ae]after generation
Toward those who fear Him.
51
He has done [af]mighty deeds with His arm;

He has scattered *those who were* proud in the [ag]thoughts of their hearts.
52
He has brought down rulers from *their* thrones,
And has exalted those who were humble.
53
He has filled the hungry with good things,
And sent the rich away empty-handed.
54
He has given help to His servant Israel,
[ah]In remembrance of His mercy,
55
Just as He spoke to our fathers,
To Abraham and his [ai]descendants forever."

56 Mary stayed with her about three months, and *then* returned to her home.

Elizabeth Gives Birth to John the Baptist

57 Now the time [aj]had come for Elizabeth to give birth, and she gave birth to a son. **58** Her neighbors and her relatives heard that the Lord had [ak]displayed His great mercy toward her; and they were rejoicing with her. **59** And it happened that on the eighth day they came to circumcise the child, and they were going to call him Zechariah, [al]after his father. **60** And *yet* his mother responded and said, "No indeed; but he shall be called John." **61** And they said to her, "There is no one among your relatives who is called by this name." **62** And they [am]made signs to his father, as to what he wanted him called. **63** And he asked for a tablet and wrote [an]as follows, "His name is John." And they were all amazed.

Zechariah Regains His Voice and Prophesies

64 And at once his mouth was opened and his tongue *freed*, and he *began* speaking in praise of God. **65** And fear came on all those who lived around them; and all these matters were being talked about in the entire hill country of Judea. **66** All who heard *them* kept *them* in mind, saying, "What then will this child *turn out to* be?" For indeed the hand of the Lord was with him.

67 And his father Zechariah was filled with the Holy Spirit and prophesied, saying:

68

"Blessed *be* the Lord God of Israel,

For He has visited *us* and accomplished redemption for His people,

69

And has raised up a horn of salvation for us

In the house of His servant David—

70

Just as He spoke by the mouth of His holy prophets from ancient times—

71

[ao]Salvation from our enemies,

And from the hand of all who hate us;

72

To show mercy to our fathers,

And to remember His holy covenant,

73

The oath which He swore to our father Abraham,

74

To grant us that we, being rescued from the hand of *our* enemies,

Would serve Him without fear,

75

In holiness and righteousness before Him all our days.

76

And you, child, also will be called the prophet of the Most High;

For you will go on before the Lord to prepare His ways;

77

To give His people *the* knowledge of salvation

[ap]By the forgiveness of their sins,

78
Because of the tender mercy of our God,
With which the Sunrise from on high will visit us,
79
To shine on those who sit in darkness and the shadow of death,
To guide our feet into the way of peace."
80 Now the child grew and was becoming strong in spirit, and he lived in the deserts until the day of his public appearance to Israel.

The Decree of Caesar Augustus

2 Now in those days a decree went out from Caesar Augustus, that a census be taken of all [aq]the inhabited earth. **2** [ar]This was the first census taken while [as]Quirinius was governor of Syria. **3** And all *the people* were on their way to register for the census, each to his own city. **4** Now Joseph also went up from Galilee, from the city of Nazareth, to Judea, to the city of David which is called Bethlehem, because he was of the house and family of David, **5** in order to register along with Mary, who was [at]betrothed to him, and was pregnant.

Jesus is Born in Bethlehem
and Wrapped in Cloths

6 While they were there, the [au]time came for her to give birth. **7** And she gave birth to her firstborn son; and she wrapped Him in cloths, and laid Him in a [av]manger, because there was no [aw]room for them in the inn.

Angels Visit the Shepherds

8 In the same region there were *some* shepherds staying out in the fields and keeping watch over their flock at night. **9** And an angel of the Lord *suddenly* stood near them, and the glory of the Lord shone around them; and they were terribly frightened. **10** And *so* the angel said to them, "Do not be afraid; for behold, I bring you good news of great joy which will be for all the people; **11** for today in the city of David there has been born for you a Savior, who is [ax]Christ the Lord. **12** And this *will be* a sign for you: you will find a baby wrapped in cloths and lying in a [ay]manger." **13** And suddenly there appeared with the angel a multitude of the heavenly [az]army *of angels* praising God and saying,

14

"Glory to God in the highest,
And on earth peace among people [ba]with whom He is pleased."

The Shepherds Find Jesus and Spread the News

15 When the angels had departed from them into heaven, the shepherds *began* saying to one another, "Let's go straight to Bethlehem, then, and see this thing that has happened, which the Lord has made known to us." **16** And they came in a hurry and found their way to Mary and Joseph, and the baby as He lay in the [bb]manger. **17** When they had seen *Him*, they made known the statement which had been told them about this Child. **18** And all who heard it were amazed about the things which were told them by the shepherds. **19** But Mary treasured all these things, pondering them in her heart. **20** And the shepherds went back, glorifying and praising God for all that they had heard and seen, just as had been told them.

21 And when eight days were completed [bc]so that it was time for His circumcision, He was also named Jesus, the *name* given by the angel before He was conceived in the womb.

Jesus Presented at the Temple and a Sacrifice Offered

22 And when the days for [bd]their purification according to the Law of Moses were completed, they brought Him up to Jerusalem to present Him to the Lord **23** (as it is written in the Law of the Lord: "Every *firstborn* male that opens the womb shall be called holy to the

Lord"), **24** and to offer a sacrifice according to what has been stated in the Law of the Lord: "A pair of turtledoves or two young doves."

The Prophecy of Simeon

25 And there was a man in Jerusalem whose name was Simeon; and this man was righteous and devout, looking forward to the consolation of Israel; and the Holy Spirit was upon him. **26** And it had been revealed to him by the Holy Spirit that he would not see death before he had seen the Lord's [be]Christ. **27** And he came [bf]by the Spirit into the temple; and when the parents brought in the child Jesus, [bg]to carry out for Him the custom of the Law, **28** then he took Him in his arms, and blessed God, and said,
29
"Now, Lord, You are letting Your bond-servant depart in peace,
According to Your word;
30
For my eyes have seen Your salvation,
31
Which You have prepared in the presence of all the peoples:
32
A light for revelation [bh]for the Gentiles,
And the glory of Your people Israel."
33 And His father and mother were amazed at the things which were being said about Him. **34** And Simeon blessed them and said to His mother Mary, "Behold, this *Child* is appointed for the fall and [bi]rise of many in Israel, and as a sign to be [bj]opposed— **35** and a sword will pierce your own soul—to the end that thoughts from many hearts may be revealed."

The Prophetess Anna Praises Jesus

36 And there was a prophetess, [bk]Anna, the daughter of Phanuel, of the tribe of Asher. She was advanced in [bl]years and had lived with *her* husband for seven years after her [bm]marriage, **37** and *then* as a widow to the age of eighty-four. She did not leave the temple *grounds*, serving night and day with fasts and prayers. **38** And at that very [bn]moment she came up and *began* giving thanks to God, and continued to speak about Him to all those who were looking forward to the redemption of Jerusalem.

Mary and Joseph Return to Nazereth with Jesus

39 And when *His parents* had completed everything in accordance with the Law of the Lord, they returned to Galilee, to their own city of Nazareth. **40** Now the Child continued to grow and to become strong.[1]

a Luke 1:1 Or *on which there is full conviction*
b Luke 1:2 Lit *became*
c Luke 1:2 Or *ministers*
d Luke 1:2 I.e., gospel
e Luke 1:3 Or *followed*
f Luke 1:4 Lit *words*
g Luke 1:4 Or *orally instructed in*
h Luke 1:5 Gr *Abia*
i Luke 1:5 I.e., of priestly descent
j Luke 1:7 Lit *days*
k Luke 1:12 Lit *fell upon*

---

1. It is my intent to comply with the NASB copyright permission in quoting the Christmas passages from the Gospels of Matthew and Luke, which is as follows:
Permission to Quote the NASB
The text of the NASB® (New American Standard Bible®) may be quoted in any form (written, visual, electronic, or audio) up to and inclusive of one thousand (1,000) verses without express written permission of The Lockman Foundation, providing the verses do not amount to a complete book of the Bible, nor do the verses quoted account for more than 50% of the total text of the work in which they are quoted, nor may more than 1,000 verses be stored in an electronic retrieval system.
Notice of copyright must appear as follows, unless otherwise stated below, on the title page, copyright page, or the section where the quoted material appears:
"Scripture quotations taken from the (NASB®) New American Standard Bible®, Copyright © 1960, 1971, 1977, 1995, 2020 by The Lockman Foundation. Used by permission. All rights reserved. lockman.org"
Only use the last year corresponding to the edition(s) quoted. For example, if quotations are from the NASB 1995, do not include the year 2020 in the copyright notice.

CHRISTMAS SCRIPTURE

l <u>Luke 1:13</u> Lit *call his name*
m <u>Luke 1:15</u> Lit *still from his*
n <u>Luke 1:18</u> Lit *days*
o <u>Luke 1:19</u> Lit *stand beside*
p <u>Luke 1:22</u> Possibly gesturing or nodding to them
q <u>Luke 1:24</u> Or *hidden*
r <u>Luke 1:27</u> Unlike engagement, a betrothed couple was considered married, but did not yet live together
s <u>Luke 1:27</u> Lit *house*
t <u>Luke 1:27</u> Gr *Mariam*, Heb *Miriam*; so throughout Luke
u <u>Luke 1:28</u> Or *be*
v <u>Luke 1:34</u> Lit *do not know a man*
w <u>Luke 1:35</u> Lit *the holy one fathered*
x <u>Luke 1:36</u> Lit *this is the sixth month for her who*
y <u>Luke 1:39</u> Lit *in these days*
z <u>Luke 1:43</u> Lit *from where this to me*
a <u>Luke 1:45</u> Or *believed, because there will be*
b <u>Luke 1:45</u> Lit *from*
c <u>Luke 1:46</u> Lit *makes great*
d <u>Luke 1:48</u> Or *consider*
e <u>Luke 1:50</u> Lit *and*
f <u>Luke 1:51</u> Lit *might*
g <u>Luke 1:51</u> Lit *thought, attitude*
h <u>Luke 1:54</u> Lit *So as to remember*
i <u>Luke 1:55</u> Lit *seed*
j <u>Luke 1:57</u> Lit *was fulfilled*
k <u>Luke 1:58</u> Lit *magnified His mercy with her*
l <u>Luke 1:59</u> Lit *after the name of*
m <u>Luke 1:62</u> I.e., gestured or nodded
n <u>Luke 1:63</u> Lit *saying*
o <u>Luke 1:71</u> Or *Deliverance*
p <u>Luke 1:77</u> Or *Consisting in*
q <u>Luke 2:1</u> I.e., the Roman Empire
r <u>Luke 2:2</u> Or *This took place as a first census*
s <u>Luke 2:2</u> Gr *Kyrenios*

t Luke 2:5 Unlike engagement, a betrothed couple was considered married, but did not yet live together
u Luke 2:6 Lit *days were completed*
v Luke 2:7 Or *feeding trough*
w Luke 2:7 Or *space*
x Luke 2:11 I.e., the Messiah
y Luke 2:12 Or *feeding trough*
z Luke 2:13 Or *host*
a Luke 2:14 Lit *of good pleasure*; or *of goodwill*
b Luke 2:16 Or *feeding trough*
c Luke 2:21 Lit *so as to circumcise Him*
d Luke 2:22 I.e., Mary's, with Joseph's support
e Luke 2:26 I.e., Messiah
f Luke 2:27 Or *in*
g Luke 2:27 Lit *to do for Him according to*
h Luke 2:32 Lit *of the Gentiles*
i Luke 2:34 Or *resurrection*
j Luke 2:34 Or *refused*
k Luke 2:36 Or *Hannah*
l Luke 2:36 Lit *days*
m Luke 2:36 Lit *virginity*
n Luke 2:38 Lit *hour*

www.ingramcontent.com/pod-product-compliance
Lightning Source LLC
Chambersburg PA
CBHW051747040426
42446CB00007B/250